AMERICAN BIRDS

American Birds

A LITERARY COMPANION

EDITED BY

Andrew Rubenfeld

AND

Terry Tempest Williams

LIBRARY OF AMERICA

Some of the material in this volume is reprinted with the permission of holders
of copyright and publishing rights. Acknowledgments are on page 251.

Distributed to the trade in the United States by Penguin Random House Inc.
and in Canada by Penguin Random House Canada Ltd.

Library of Congress Control Number: 2019943291
ISBN 978–1–59853–655–3

1 3 5 7 9 10 8 6 4 2

Printed in the United States of America

Contents

Thomas Merton's Ravens
William Merwin's Meadowlark

BY TERRY TEMPEST WILLIAMS

WHAT IS THE DATE? It doesn't matter. What is the time? My shadow is by my side. It is early spring, the dried leaves of cottonwoods are a reminder of what has been. I am sitting on sand the color of my skin and it comforts me. The valley we live in is quiet—save for a buzz saw I can hear in the background. Somewhere someone is building something. The gathering clouds are alerting me not to be seduced for long by the glory of this day—a sky the color of lapis against the red rock cliffs is suddenly interrupted by the wing beats of ravens.

I look up. Two ravens circle above me. Their familiar caw reminds me there are other beings who live here beyond my own kind. They are in conversation even in flight. I am tempted to join them and I do, raising my voice with theirs. They come closer spiraling around each other—rising—circling—falling.

Now there are three. Count me as four. They caw. I respond. My voice is met by their caws and I become bolder, braver, my voice more closely mimicking the ravens' voices. They widen their circle, three more ravens join them. Six ravens above me, now seven—and then, the seven ravens transform themselves into one before my very eyes. Now a single Raven circles above me, close enough to touch.

Trickster.

We call back and forth. Eye contact is made—so close—the Raven appears iridescent in the afternoon sun. I take off my ring, silver and shiny, and hold it up as an offering, a glint of light that captures her eye.

My Aunt Mattie would approve as it was her turquoise ring framed with intricate silver Florentine petals that she wore in the years she lived on the Navajo Reservation in the 1940s. She bequeathed it to me when I was seven years old.

And then, the Raven disappears. Silence. Stillness. Until a rush of white-crowned sparrows fills the void, landing in the bare cottonwood trees whose exposed roots are clinging to the edge of the wash.

I am left alone.

Do you suppose I have a spiritual life? I have none. I am indigence. I am silence. I am poverty. I am solitude, for I have renounced spirituality to find God, and He it is who preaches loudly in the depths of my indulgence saying: "I will pour out my spirit upon thy children and they shall spring up among the herbs as willows beside the running waters." —Thomas Merton

What do I believe? I believe in this moment, this desert, this wind, this sand upon which I sit that was brought here by the torrents of Placid Creek last fall. I remember that night, the roar and the rumbling of the water. I heard fear first before I stepped outside and witnessed the flash flood running deep and cutting fast into the narrow arroyo close to our home, widening as boulders and juniper trees swept past, carried away by a storm that gathered and spilled many miles upriver that we never knew was coming. When the rushing water stilled and settled across the desert, it became a broken mirror reflecting moonlight.

And I heard ravens circling above.

Such curious birds of darkness and light.

But now, they are gone and I am left with silence. Make that plural. Silences. I hear them and take them into my body like water.

Ravens farther north, when they talk, mimic water.

I was not sure where I was going, and I could not see what I would do when I got [there]. But you saw further and clearer than I . . . whose track led me across the waters to a place I had never dreamed of, and which you were even then preparing to be my rescue and my shelter and my home.
                                                              —Thomas Merton

I have long believed that birds are mediators between heaven and earth. They precede a birth, they foretell a death, I worship them.

Many years ago, on the shores of Great Salt Lake, Utah's inland sea, I prayed to the birds at a time when I needed solace over the death of my mother and grandmothers. I still pray to them. *I pray to the birds because I believe they will carry the messages of my heart upward. I pray to them because I believe in their existence, the way their songs begin and end each day—the invocations and benedictions of Earth. I pray to the birds because they remind me of what I love rather than what I fear. And at the end of my prayers, they teach me how to listen.*   —*Refuge*

This morning, I awoke to the song of a meadowlark, the first of this season. I went outside and saw my hope standing on the top of sage. The meadowlark turned and in full sunlight flashed its victorious yellow breast against the red rocks, blue sky, reminding me of all things primary. Joy filled the valley. Ravens appeared once again.

A few moments later, a friend called to tell me of the poet William Merwin's death.

I paused to take in the news as the tears came. He was my friend, my mentor, our greatest poet, who not only wrote poetry but planted palms on the land he and his wife Paula restored on the island of Maui. All at once, the world felt less safe, less wise, less everything— and I recalled a line from his poem "The Estuary": "We are asleep with compasses in our hands."

Birds awaken us, guide us, direct us to our own attention. Paying attention is what William Merwin taught me repeatedly. I remember a time when he called me into his study. My brother had just died from lymphoma. I had been listening to owls. I was heartbroken, wearing my grief openly. Merwin looked at me and dispassionately said, "This is the place we write from." He then invited me to sit with him in silence in his meditation room.

It is appropriate that this exquisite anthology, *American Birds: A Literary Companion*, published by Library of America, should end with "Unknown Bird" by W. S. Merwin. The poet writes, "where is it from / hardly anyone / seems to have noticed it / so far but who now /

would have been listening"—and two stanzas down continues, "so keeps on calling for / no one who is here / hoping to be heard."

It is time to listen to the birds and hear what they have to say to us. It is our turn to give something back to the birds who have given so much to us humans through the millennia.

We are losing them—species by species—long-legged birds like the Eskimo curlew, the dusky seaside sparrow, and the rare Everglade kite. We are no longer seeing the willow flycatcher on the banks of the Colorado River as we once did. Nor are we seeing redheads and canvasbacks in the numbers we once did in the marshes of the Great Salt Lake. We can no longer take the most common of species for granted. Imagine a world without robins. Let these pages, written through the ages of our country's history, not become an elegy, but a literary point of advocacy for the beauty and enduring grace of birds, the eternal surprise of their presence as they migrate through the seasons, how they leave and they return in their extraordinary capacity to navigate in the dark through the guidance of stars.

Ravens, white-crowned sparrows, meadowlarks, and owls calling forth in the night remind us, as our theologians, writers, and poets do, that we do not exist without birdsong and flight.

Here in the desert, sitting on sand, the ravens cavort and caw with one another as they play on the heat waves. I wonder if they know what is coming.

Introduction

BY ANDREW RUBENFELD

THE STORIES ARE SIMILAR: that moment when it clicks, your life changes, and you become a bird watcher.

My parents had recommended the excursion to Baker Island off the coast of Maine. And they loaned me their binoculars: "You'll need them." It was the end of July and the island was full of birds that I couldn't identify. The ranger pointed out ospreys, cormorants, and terns, swallows, catbirds, and thrushes—and some smaller birds. "That warbler is getting ready to migrate south. Do you know where it might spend the winter?" A few decent guesses. "South America." I had grown up with woods behind the house, I had been a Boy Scout, but that American redstart did it. The next day my companion and I bought a second pair of binoculars and altered our itinerary to include national wildlife refuges. By the end of the trip I had seen and identified seventy species.

Americans have always been deeply aware of nature, and they have always watched birds. But the reasons for their careful observations have shifted since the first European settlers arrived. Nature in the New World was different—abundant, varied, close at hand—unlike what they had experienced at home where it had been marginalized and extirpated since Neolithic times. There wild nature was something you had to go to desolate marshes or distant mountains or forbidden forests to encounter. John Locke declared that "In the beginning all the World was America." Here was the bounty of Eden.

The colonists saw nature as essential for physical survival and as resources for trade. This commodity use is, of course, a story as old as human economic activity itself, a constant in our attitude toward the natural world. Walter Raleigh, in promoting and developing the colony at Roanoke Island, had the good sense to send two remarkable individuals—John White and Thomas Hariot—to catalogue and record this natural bounty in the 1580s. White's extraordinary watercolors depict native housing and agriculture to show that the indigenous people were not savage. Hariot, a respected Elizabethan scientist, describes natural resources such as plants, trees, minerals, fish, mammals—and birds. His *Brief and True Report of the New Found Land of Virginia* (1588) contains the earliest bird watching account in America.

> Turkie cockes and Turkie hennes: Stock doves: Partridges: Cranes: Hernes: & in winter great store of Swannes & Geese. . . . There are also Parats, Faulcons, & Marlin haukes, which although with us they bee not used for meate, yet for other causes I thought good to mention.

Similarly, William Wood, writing nearly a half century later in *New Englands Prospect* (1634), talks about these "usefull and beneficiall creatures" but adds that "The Humbird is one of the wonders of the Countrey . . . she is as glorious as the Raine-bow." Such moments of rapture could be justified by Puritan bird observers by acknowledging nature's bounty and beauty as gifts from God.

Toward the end of the colonial period gentleman farmer J. Hector St. John de Crèvecoeur also describes the ruby-throated hummingbird. While the hummingbird is for him neither a useful commodity nor its sighting an occasion for spiritual reflection, he offers a careful account of the bird. With the establishment of the new country, it was appropriate to note the abundant and varied and still proximate resources with scientific acumen matched by nationalistic pride.

In May 1804, Captains Meriwether Lewis and William Clark plus two dozen soldiers of the U.S. Corps of Discovery—as well as several interpreters, the indispensable Shoshone woman Sacagawea, Clark's personal black servant York, and Lewis's Newfoundland dog—set out from St. Louis. Following detailed instructions from President Jefferson ("the animals of the country generally, & especially those not known in the U.S. . . . the remains & accounts of any which may be rare or extinct . . . times of appearance of particular birds, reptiles or insects") and funded by Congress, Lewis and Clark were to explore the Louisiana territory recently purchased from France. By the time the expedition returned in September 1806 it had secretly (but with the president's approval) gone beyond American territory, crossing the Rockies to the Pacific coast. It had initiated, for the most part, good relations with two dozen native tribes, mapped the topography of the prairies, mountains, and rivers, and brought back numerous samples of minerals, flora, and fauna. In their extensive journals Lewis and Clark record their wonder, often delighting in birds that are new and strange and therefore needing names: Lewis's woodpecker, Clark's nutcracker, for example.

John James Audubon undertook a more modest, but no less important, voyage of discovery when in early 1820 he headed down the Ohio and Mississippi Rivers on a flatboat. His plan was to study and draw the birds of America, and ultimately to produce a work of avian verisimilitude that would surpass Alexander Wilson's recent three-volume *American Ornithology* (1807–14). He relied on his gun to acquire specimens and visited the food markets of New Orleans where hunters brought in mounds of dead birds (ducks, geese, cranes, herons, coots, godwits, snipe, plovers, doves, woodpeckers, tree swallows, blackbirds, bluebirds, robins, warblers—you name it). By the winter of 1822, Audubon was back in Kentucky trying to gain financial support to publish a folio of his engravings. In 1829 the *American Journal of Science and Arts* called the first 49 plates of *Birds of America* "the most magnificent work of its kind ever executed in any country."

In his 1836 essay *Nature*—the transcendentalist manifesto—Ralph Waldo Emerson enumerates the various uses of nature that, if practiced, will lead to philosophical and/or spiritual wholeness. The most basic use is commodity: without it you don't survive. But also integral to nature is its beauty: aesthetic, moral, and intellectual. Nature is also a vast, rich, hieroglyphic language. Discipline your life to use its resources, learn its lessons, and discover its innate meanings, and eventually you will transcend who you now are and link with the entire cosmos. This is a hands-on philosophy: immerse yourself in nature. When Emerson's younger neighbor Henry David Thoreau was a senior at Harvard College, *Nature* made a great impression on him and influenced his own later writings. *Walden* (1854), subtitled "A Life in the Woods," is his experiment poised midway between society and wildness. That book, dozens of essays, and decades of journal entries reveal Thoreau to be first and foremost a true sojourner in nature. His descriptions of birds remain unsurpassed in their beauty. Reading Emerson and Thoreau, we eavesdrop on them as they go bird watching together in the woods and fields and on the ponds of Concord, Massachusetts.

By the early nineteenth century, nature in pre-industrialized America was still abundant, varied, and close at hand. Most Americans could identify dozens of bird species, partly due to eating habits and preferences (ducks are good to eat, gulls less so). How many species can the average American identify today, with birds less numerous and no longer near most of us? But it would be naive if not misinformed to think that avian life was regarded as something inviolate. The attitude toward this American Eden was, and unfortunately still is, too often guided by unrestrained financial motives, by short-sightedness that America is big, its resources endless and self-restoring, and by a belief falsely thought to be biblically sanctioned that the natural world is there to use, even use up. Such views are evident in "On the Emigration to America and Peopling the Western Country," Philip Freneau's poem written after the Treaty of Paris gave the new United States the unsettled trans-Appalachian West:

> What charming scenes attract the eye.
> On wild Ohio's savage stream!
> There Nature reigns, whose works outvie
> The boldest pattern art can frame . . .

For the Mississippi River and its ten thousand streams, "Far other ends, the heavens decree— / And commerce plans new freights for thee." An aggressive Manifest Destiny was in the wings. The concept of stewardship would be a long way off. How could the Carolina parakeet withstand the ceaseless attacks by angry fruit growers in the South? The plentiful heath hen (the poor man's food) was no match for the agricultural blitz that swept Long Island and elsewhere along the Atlantic seaboard. Even the huge numbers of passenger pigeons could not survive wanton hunting and the destruction of contiguous acorn-bearing oak forests.

By this time nature writing—not yet environmental writing—had developed a distinct structure. Similar to Hudson River School landscape painting, it drew on firsthand observation of actual natural objects or events. There was no need to make up creatures: no dragons, no water nymphs or elves, not a phoenix or a sphinx. Notice how the details about the bird and the setting in William Cullen Bryant's waterfowl poem enable the poet to see the higher lessons gained from the experience of watching the bird. This pattern holds for many of the poems included here—by Emily Dickinson and Herman Melville (and also the story by Sarah Orne Jewett) as well as later poems by Robert Frost and Mary Oliver.

For American Indians animals, and birds in particular, were part of the material and spirit worlds, both close at hand. Ethnographic studies beginning in the mid-1800s included transcriptions into English of this rich duality. Songs by the Ojibwa from Lake Superior, the Tigua from Texas, and the Pima from the Southwest open this anthology.

Walt Whitman's Long Island boyhood brought him into intimate contact with nature. He transformed his early bird watching into poems such as "Out of the Cradle Endlessly Rocking" (mockingbird) and "When Lilacs Last in the Dooryard Bloom'd" (hermit thrush). The poet decodes the songs of these fellow "solitary singers," songs of death, love, and redemption, and offers his own. The journal selections included here record his bird watching in central New Jersey while recovering from nearly paralytic strokes after the Civil War.

Awareness and concern for an increasingly compromised environment leads to another shift in writing about birds just as it initiates the modern conservation movement in the United States. Sarah Orne Jewett's story of a "white heron" (snowy egret), unusual in Maine in the 1880s, reflects growing outrage over the slaughter of birds in Florida and elsewhere for feathers in women's hats. Bird watching should be a responsible activity, with its own set of acceptable behaviors that reflect a broader code of environmental ethics. Yet bird watching, as the celebratory sheer joy of observing these creatures, also begins here. It is democratic and free, although having a pair of opera glasses (as nature writer Florence Merriam had) and something called a field guide (thank you, Frank Chapman) help.

Twentieth-century American literature abounds in poems about birds as watching them became a favorite pastime of many people.

There are fairly traditional styles such as Robert Frost's sonnet on an ovenbird and Robinson Jeffers's free verse on a turkey vulture. Carl Sandburg is innovative about purple martins; William Carlos Williams goes minimalist about a towhee. What about the stately modernism of Marianne Moore, the delicious wit of Ogden Nash and E. B. White, the swan-shaped poem of John Hollander, the elegance of May Swenson's anhinga poem? That this book serves as a comprehensive who's who of modern American poetry underscores the ways in which birds continue to serve as powerful metaphors for beauty, escape, imagination, and spiritual transcendence.

It can be said that environmental writing, as distinct from nature writing, begins in 1864 with the publication of Thoreau's *The Maine Woods* and George Perkins Marsh's geography textbook, *Man and Nature*. It is Marsh who first understands the intricate cause-and-effect relationships, call it ecology, of the world around us. Naturalists such as John Burroughs, Theodore Roosevelt, John Muir, and others fight to save the land and the living things on it. They lobby legislators and found organizations such as the National Audubon Society, the Sierra Club, the Linnaean Society of New York. They write persuasive books and articles about conservation issues, but they also (as included here) record their personal connections to birds.

Mid-twentieth-century environmentalists continue this tradition. Before she published *Silent Spring* in 1962, Rachel Carson was well-known for a trilogy of books about the sea and the life in it and at its edges—a black skimmer makes an appearance in this anthology. Roger Tory Peterson (already a household name for eponymous field guides to the birds) and Englishman James Fisher travel around the continent in search of "wild America" (the Everglades) and Pulitzer Prize–winner Edwin Way Teale follows the seasons and the birds in a four-volume sequence (Cape May). Embracing Thoreau's "I have traveled a good deal in Concord,"

Aldo Leopold stays at home in Wisconsin to detail the zoological events of the changing seasons, such as the "sky dance" of the American woodcock.

Contemporary American bird writing, and other nature writing too, frequently has an undertone of lament for a lost world or is a sheaf of dire warnings that worse is yet to come. Hopeful bird watchers dream about recreating the DNA of the ivory-billed woodpecker just as they are aware that a warming North American climate will cause the Bicknell's thrush to go extinct in a few years. The loss and fragmentation of habitat for migratory and resident birds due to monoculture farming or deleted forests or another suburban shopping mall is a familiar refrain. Are we witnessing the beginning of the end of nature?

Yet despite these very real and scary gloom-and-doom scenarios now and to come, much of American bird writing remains alert, and even celebratory. And quirky. Compare Sidney Lanier's dutiful 1891 sonnet about a mockingbird with Randall Jarrell's fairly straightforward 1965 account. Then look at David Martinez's 2014 poem about a bird that "croons a tune from his / pompadour and beak." Would Crèvecoeur recognize Lorna Dee Cervantes's hummingbirds "stuck to each other"? Cornelius Eady's crows: Are they birds or a metaphor for humans dancing—why not both? Jack Collom's "Ruddy Duck" abounds in off-the-scale enthusiasm and maybe off-the-wall nuttiness.

Owl lovers: here's a batch of recent poems by Charles Simic (great horned owl), Duane Niatum (snowy owl), Richard Wilbur (barred owl), and Ted Kooser (screech owl). Consider the impressive array of startling details for David Wagoner's kingfisher, Mary Oliver's gannets, Pamela Uschuk's snow geese, and Timothy Steele's black phoebe. You can smell the Aleutian crags and hear the raucous calls and the pummeling water in Emily Wilson's "Red-Legged Kittiwake." For evocative visual and auditory images: the swirling cliff swallows in Debra Nystrom's poem, the tonal spectrum of Sidney Wade's indigo bunting, and the "quicksilver trill" of the cactus wren described by Ursula K. Le Guin. For bird–human interaction there is the bittersweetness of Mark Jarman's scarlet tanager poem and a New York City office worker's sudden encounter with a peregrine falcon in Robert Cording's poem.

Today's prose writers also capture the troubled joys of bird watching. In *Red-Tails in Love*, Marie Winn gives us a portrait of Pale Male, a genuine New York City celebrity with features so distinctive that he could always be identified over Central Park or at his Fifth Avenue high-rise nest. For Terry Tempest Williams, looking at birds around the Great Salt Lake became itself a "refuge" as she observed the area's ecological fragility and, more poignantly, the incidence of breast cancer in her family. Richard Powers sets his novel *The Echo Maker* near the Platte River in Nebraska, where the sandhill cranes are integrally woven into the fabric of the narrative. Jonathan Rosen says that the "urge to watch birds is all but instinctive" and that observing birds "is as human an activity as there can be." In 2015, Noah Strycker set out to do a global "big year." When he briefly returned to the United States midtrip he had to reassess one kind of birding—rarity chasing—and wonder what modern bird watching itself is all about.

In *Life Is a Miracle* (2000), Wendell Berry records his joy at watching birds from his study window in Kentucky, something he has done for much of his adult life.

> I saw four wood ducks riding the current, apparently for fun. A great blue heron was fishing, standing in the water up to his belly feathers. Through binoculars I saw him stoop forward, catch, and swallow a fish. At the feeder

on the window sill, goldfinches, titmice, chickadees, nuthatches, and cardinals have been busy at a heap of free (to
them) sunflower seeds. A flock of crows has found something newsworthy in the cornfield across the river.

Few writers have been as dedicated as Berry to knowing a particular
place and knowing it very well, so that his pleasure always comes
tinged with the awareness that "This is a small, fragile place" and
that "in two hours a bulldozer could make it unrecognizable to me,
and perfectly recognizable to every 'developer.'" The pleasures and
pains that we have in watching birds—and that by extension we take
in reading about them—must be tempered by concern and action,
both big and small, in preserving the places critical to their survival.
The "strange stillness" that Rachel Carson describes in *Silent Spring*
is always nearby and, without our continuing vigilance, here.

This anthology gathers some of the best American bird writing,
both prose and verse, from the colonial period to the present. It
is arranged chronologically by the date of first publication or (for
journal entries) by the date of composition, with two notable excep-
tions—the transcriptions of American Indian songs that begin the
anthology and the Merwin poem that concludes it. In making our
selections we have followed three principles. First, we have avoided
ornithological writings in favor of literary works that emphasize
vivid personal encounters with birds. Second, we have tried to
represent a wide range of bird species in the anthology, but these
selections can only begin to suggest the rich diversity of species
and ecosystems in America. Third, we have attempted to represent
a gamut of writing styles and concerns. Here again, necessarily, we

can only begin to gesture toward something much larger—the rich terrain of American writing inspired by birds that we hope readers will want to explore further on their own.

Three American Indian Songs About Birds

HAWK CHANT OF THE SAGINAWS (OJIBWA)

The hawks turn their heads nimbly round;
They turn to look back on their flight.
The spirits of sun-place have whispered them words,
They fly with their messages swift,
They look as they fearfully go,
They look to the farthermost end of the world,
Their eyes glancing bright, and their beaks boding harm.

FROM HENRY ROWE SCHOOLCRAFT, *INDIAN TRIBES OF THE UNITED STATES* (1853)

THE MOCKING-BIRD'S SONG (TIGUA)

Rain, people, rain!
The rain is all around us.
It is going to come pouring down,
And the summer will be fair to see,
The mocking-bird has said so.

FROM ALICE C. FLETCHER, *INDIAN STORY AND SONG
FROM NORTH AMERICA* (1900)

THE ROAD-RUNNER (PIMA)

Road-Runner with the crested head
Goes crying poi, poi,
As he runs around the house,
Poi, poi, all around the house.

Here is the lonely road-runner
Poi, poi, the lonely road-runner,
He eats lizards in the morning,
He eats solitary lizards.

Here is the red-eyed road-runner,
Poi, poi, the red-eyed road-runner
Who runs about the mistletoe,
This is the red-eyed road-runner.

I run and hide
I run and hide,
Now I kill gray lizard,
His fat body I eat up.
  I run and hide,
  I run and hide
  In the garramboya bush.

FROM MARY AUSTIN, *THE CHILDREN SING IN THE*
  FAR WEST (1928)

J. Hector St. John de Crèvecoeur

ON THE HUMMING BIRD (1782)

ONE OF MY CONSTANT walks when I am at leisure, is in my low-lands, where I have the pleasure of seeing my cattle, horses, and colts. Exuberant grass replenishes all my fields, the best representative of our wealth; in the middle of that track I have cut a ditch eight feet wide, the banks of which nature adorns every spring with the wild salendine, and other flowering weeds, which on these luxuriant grounds shoot up to a great height. Over this ditch I have erected a bridge, capable of bearing a loaded waggon; on each side I carefully sow every year, some grains of hemp, which rise to the height of fifteen feet, so strong and so full of limbs as to resemble young trees: I once ascended one of them four feet above the ground. These produce natural arbours, rendered often still more compact by the assistance of an annual creeping plant which we call a vine, that never fails to entwine itself among their branches, and always produces a very desirable shade. From this simple grove I have amused myself an hundred times in observing the great number of humming birds with which our country abounds: the wild blossoms every where attract the attention of these birds, which like bees subsist by suction. From this retreat I distinctly watch them in all their various attitudes; but their flight is so rapid, that you cannot distinguish the motion of their wings. On this little bird nature has profusely lavished her most splendid colours; the most perfect azure, the most beautiful gold, the most dazzling red, are for ever in contrast, and help to embellish the plumes of his majestic head.

The richest pallet of the most luxuriant painter, could never invent any thing to be compared to the variegated tints, with which this insect bird is arrayed. Its bill is as long and as sharp as a coarse sewing needle; like the bee, nature has taught it to find out in the calix of flowers and blossoms, those mellifluous particles that serve it for sufficient food; and yet it seems to leave them untouched, undeprived of any thing that our eyes can possibly distinguish. When it feeds, it appears as if immoveable, though continually on the wing; and sometimes, from what motives I know not, it will tear and lacerate flowers into a hundred pieces: for, strange to tell, they are the most irascible of the feathered tribe. Where do passions find room in so diminutive a body? They often fight with the fury of lions, until one of the combatants falls a sacrifice and dies. When fatigued, it has often perched within a few feet of me, and on such favourable opportunities I have surveyed it with the most minute attention. Its little eyes appear like diamonds, reflecting light on every side: most elegantly finished in all parts it is a miniature work of our great parent who seems to have formed it the smallest, and at the same time the most beautiful of the winged species.

Meriwether Lewis and William Clark

FROM *JOURNALS*, 1805–1806

JUNE 4, 1805 (LEWIS)

IN THESE PLAINS I observed great numbers of the brown Curloos, a small species of curloo or plover of a brown colour about the size of the common snipe and not unlike it in form with a long celindric curved and pointed beak; it's wings are proportionately long and the tail short; in the act of liteing this bird lets itself down by an extention of it's wings without motion holding their points very much together above it's back, in this rispect differing ascentially from any bird I ever observed.   a number of sparrows also of three distinct species I observed.   also a small bird which in action resembles the lark, it is about the size of a large sparrow of a dark brown colour with some white fathers in the tail; this bird or that which I take to be the male rises into the air about 60 feet and supporting itself in the air with a brisk motion of the wings sings very sweetly, has several shrill soft notes reather of the plaintive order which it frequently repeats and varies, after remaining stationary about a minute in his aireal station he descends obliquely occasionly pausing and accomnying his decension with a note something like *twit twit twit*; on the ground he is silent.   thirty or forty of these birds will be stationed in the air at a time in view, these larks as I shall call them add much to the gayety and cheerfullness of the scene. All those birds are now seting and laying their eggs in the plains; their little nests are to be seen in great abundance as we pass.

MARCH 2, 1806 (CLARK)

The *Heath Cock* or *cock of the Plains* is found in the Plains of Columbia and are in great abundance from the enterance of Lewis's river to the mountains which pass the Columbia between the Great falls and Rapids of that river. this fowl is about ¾ths the Size of a turkey. the beak is large Short Curved and convex. the upper exceeding the lower chap. the nostrils are large and the back black. the Colour is a uniform mixture of dark brown reather bordering on a dove colour, redish and yellowish brown with Some Small black Specks. in this mixture the dark brown provails and has a Slight cast of the dove colour at a little distance. the wider side of the larger feathers of the wings are of a dark brown only. the tail is composed of 19 feathers of which that in the center is the longest, and the remaining 9 on each Side deminish by pairs as they receede from the Center; that is any one feather is equal in length to one of an equal distance from the Center of the tail on the opposit Side. the tail when folded Comes to a very Sharp point and appears long in perpotion to the body in the act of flying the tail resembles that of a wild pigeon. tho' the motion of the wings is much that of the Pheasant and Grouse. they have four toes on each foot of which the hinder one is Short. the leg is covered with feathers about half the distance between the knee and foot. when the wings is expanded there are wide opening between it's feathers, the plumage being So narrow that it does not extend from one quill to another. the wings are also propotionably Short, reather more So than those of the Pheasant or Grouse. the habits of this bird is much the Same as those of the Prarie hen or Grouse. only that the food of this fowl is almost entirely that of the leaf and buds of the pulpy leafed thorn, nor do I ever recollect Seeing this bird but in the neighbourhood of that Shrub. The gizzard of it is large and

Grouse are about short and eye.

Cock cock which on the and hood Mountains to the Mountain the Columbia the great falls they go in large or singularly

the feathers about its head pointed and stiff Some hairs the base of the beak. feathers fine and stiff about the ears.

This is a faint likeness of the of the plains or Heath

the flesh of those fowls we met with was Missourie below in the neighbour of the Rocky and from which pass between and Rapids gorges and make

hide hide remarkably close when pursued.

short flights &c.

The large Black & white Pheasant is peculiar to that portion of the Rocky Mountains watered by the Columbia River. at least we did not see them untill we reached the waters of that river, nor since we have left those mountains. they are about the size of a well grown hen. the contour of the bird is much that of the redish brown Pheasant common to our country. the tail is proportionably as long and is composed of 18 feathers of equal length. of a uniform dark brown tiped with black. the feathers of the are of a dark brown black and white. the black much less compressed and muscular than in most fowls, in Short it resembles a maw quite as much as a gizzard. When they fly they make a cackling noise Something like the dunghill fowl.   the flesh of this fowl is dark and only tolerable in point of flavour.   I do not think it as good as wth the Pheasant or Prarie hen, or Grouse.   the feathers above it's head are pointed and Stiff Some hairs about the base of the beak.   feathers Short fine and Stiff about the ears, and eye. This is a faint likeness of the *Cock* of the plains or Heath Cock.   the first of those fowls which we met with was on the Missouri below and in the neighbourhood of the Rocky Mountains and from to the mountain which passes the Columbia between the Great falls and Rapids they go in large gangues or Singularly and hide remarkably close when pursued, make Short flights, &c.

The large Black & White *Pheasant* is peculiar to that portion of the Rocky Mountains watered by the Columbia River.   at least we did not See them untill we reached the waters of that river, nor Since we have left those mountains.   they are about the Size of a well grown hen.   the contour of the bird is much that of the redish brown Pheasant common to our country.   the tail is proportionably as long and is composed of 18 feathers of equal length, of a uniform dark brown tiped with black.   the feathers of the body are of a dark brown black and white.   the black is that which most prodomonates, and white feathers are irregularly intermixed with those of the black and dark brown on every part but in greater perpotion about the neck breast and belly.   this mixture gives it very much the appearance of that kind of dunghill fowl, which the hen-wives of our Countrey Call *dommanicker.*   in the brest of Some of those birds the white prodominates most.   they are not furnished with tufts of long feathers on the neck as other Pheasants are, but have a Space on each Side of the neck about 2½ inches long and one inch in width on which no feathers grow, tho' it is consealed by the feathers which are inserted on the hinder and front part of the neck, this Space Seams to Serve them to dilate or contract the feathers of the neck with more ease.   the eye is dark, the beak black, uncovered Somewhat pointed and the upper exceeds the under chap.   they have a narrow Strip of vermillion colour above each eye which consists of a fleshey Substance not protuberant but uneaven, with a number of minute rounded dots.   it has four toes on each foot of which three are in front, it is booted to the toes.   it feeds on wild fruits, particularly the berry of the *Sac-a-com-mis*, and much also on the Seed of the pine & fir.   this fowl is usially found in Small numbers two and three & 4 together on the ground.   when Supprised flies up & lights on a tree and is easily Shot.   their flesh is Superior to most of the Pheasant Species which we have met with.   they have a gizzard as other Pheasants &c.   feed also on the buds of the Small Huckleberry bushes.

May 27, 1806 (Lewis)

The Black woodpecker which I have frequently mentioned and which is found in most parts of the roky Mountains as well as the Western and S. W. mountains. I had never an opportunity of examining untill a few days since when we killed and preserved several of them.   this bird is about the size of the lark woodpecker or the turtle dove, tho' it's wings are longer than either of those birds.   the beak is black, one inch long, reather wide at the base, somewhat curved, and sharply pointed; the chaps are of equal length.   arround the base of the beak including the eye and a small part of the throat is of a fine crimson red.   the neck and as low as the croop in front is of an iron grey.   the belly and breast is a curious mixture of white and blood reed which has much the appearance of having been artifically painted or stained of that colour.   the red reather predominates.   the top of the head back, sides, upper surface of the wings and tail are black, with a glossey tint of green in a certain exposure to the light. the under side of the wings and tail are of a sooty black. it has ten feathers in the tail, sharply pointed, and those in the center reather longest, being 2 ½ inches in length. the tongue is barbed, pointed, and of an elastic cartelaginous substance. the eye is moderately large, puple black and iris of a dark yellowish brown. this bird in it's actions when flying resembles the small redheaded woodpecke common to the Atlantic states; it's note also somewhat resembles that bird. the pointed tail seems to assist it in seting with more eas or retaining it its resting position against the perpendicular side of a tree. the legs and feet are black and covered with wide imbricated scales. it has four toes on each foot of which two are in rear and two in front; the nails are much curved long and remarkably keen or sharply pointed. it feeds on bugs worms and a variety of insects.

John James Audubon

FROM *MISSISSIPPI RIVER JOURNAL*, 1820–1821

NOVEMBER 12, 1820

The Wind Blowed this Morning and We did Not Leave the Shore untill 9 'oclock—Wind fair—weather, raw & Cloudy—Mr *Aumack* killed a Duck (Ruddy Duck) out of a Flock of 5 that proved to be a *Nondescript*—and also a *Imber Diver*—the Wind rendered our Cabin smoaky   I Could Not begin to Draw untill after Dinner—I had the Pleasure of Seing Two of the Same Ducks Swimming Deep, with their Tail *erect*, and Diving for food = having never seen these Birds before, it was highly satisfactorily to Me = Tomorrow I will give a thorough Description of it =

The *Imber Diver* was Shot Dead and proved a beautifull specimen—of Course I will give You a Drawing of it—for Some time before I procured one of them; they Were Called *Northern Divers*, the Moment I saw this, the size and Coloring Made Me Sure of it being an *Imber Diver*—

saw a Large flock of Turkeys fly across from an Island to the Main, killed None—

We are Landed about half a Mile above the *Cumberland Island*   the weather not So cold as it feels   the Thermometer at 38—had some spits of Snow in the forenoon—

Vast flocks of Ducks & Geese flying Southwardly—

NOVEMBER 14, 1820

Drawing this Morning as soon as the Light would permit me—
Started early—

Went out in the Skiff to try to Shoot the *Largest* White *Crane* with
Black tips, but I walk^d off from the Shore and I return^d knowing
that it would be vain to attempt to follow him on a Large naked
Sand Barr—felt great anxiety to procure Such for he appeared
Beautifull—

Saw several Eagles, *Brown* & White *headed*—

Although I drew nearly the Whole of this day I did finished my
Imber Diver.

———————◆———————

Total Length of the Fin Tailed Duck 15½ Inches—¾ Hinds Shorter
to Side of Tail   Bill Dark Blue   Broad for the size of the Bird—&
Sharply hook^d at the point—Legs & feet L. Blue the palms Black,
Tang Fleshy—upper Part of the Head Back Wings & Tail Dark Brown
Zig Zags with transversal Bars of Light D°—Irides Dark Chestnut
Eye rather Small   Neck Breast & Belly Light Brown with transver-
sal Black Drops—a Triangular White Spot forming the under Tail
Coverts—

Tail Composed of 18 Feathers rounding   each feather narrow
Sharp & Terminating in Spoon Like Shape points—this is White—
the Head & Neck Short and Thick—

Swims Deep   White part of the Belly Silvery White—

Breadth 22 Inches—Wings Brown Not reaching the Tail by ½
Inch—No Wing Stripes—

When I saw these Birds the Weather was Boisterous   since fair
have not Seen One—

Imber Diver Weighed	6 lb.	
Total Length	2 $^{8}/_{12}$	feet—
to end of Tail	2 $^{4\frac{1}{2}}/_{12}$	—"—
Width tip to tip	4	—"—
Length of the Gut	5 $^{8}/_{12}$	—"—

Contents of Gutt & Gizard Small Fish, Bones & Scales and Large Gravel—Body extremely fat & rancid—Belly & Vest White but Not silvery as in the Grebes—

NOVEMBER 23, 1820

as soon as We had eat our *Common Breakfast,* fried Bacon and Soaked Biskuit—Joseph went to his station and I to Mine, i.e. he rowed the Skiff and I steering it—Went to the *Litle Prairie* shot at a Brown Eagle probably 250 Yards and Yet Cut one of its Legs—

at this Place We Saw a great Number of Birds, Mostly *Red Breasted Thrushes*—the Songs of Which revived our Spirits and Imparted Within us the Sweet sensation that Spring brings to Minds of *our Kind.*

the Rusty Grakles extremely Plenty—snow Birds—& Many Sparows—

I Shot a Beautifull *White headed Eagle Falco Leucocephalus*—probably 150 Yards off, My Ball Went through its body—

Returned to our Boats immediatly and began My Drawing—it is a Handsome Male—

Many Shots at Geese, but We find them so Shy that We Loose Much Ammunition in Contending With them—

floated 23 Miles   Landed Opposite Island Nº 20 according to the Old Navigator, some Indians Camped on it, Made us Load all our pieces—

I saw Two Eagles Nest, One of them I remembered seing as I went to New Orleans 18 Months ago   it had being worked upon and No doubt Youngs Where raised in it, it is in a Large Cypress Tree, Not very high, Made of Very Large & Dead Sticks and about 8 feet in Diameter—

Since I killed the One before me I am Convinced that the *Bald Eagle* and the *Brown Eagle* are Two Diferent Species—

November 24, 1820

high Winds, remained at our Last Night's harbour all day—at Day Break saw a Deer Crossing the River below us, ran him down and Brought him to the Boats; Cleaned, it Weighed 162^{lb} had 9 Points to its horns and so Much run down that its Neck Was swolen ½ the Size of its Body—

I Spent the greater Part of the day drawing; all hands hunting—Killed Two Geese, 1 Racoon & 1 Oppossum—

the Woods here are so Dreadfully tangled with *Bull rushes*, Green Briars and Canes that the Travelling through them is extremely Irksome =

saw some *Carrion Crows* and some *Turkey Buzards* that were attracted by the scent?? of the Deer we had hung in the Woods??—

saw some Ivory Billed Wood Peckers, these Birds allways go in Paires and When they Leave a Tree to fly to another they Sail and Look not unlike a *Raven*—I shot & killed a Turkey Buzzard a great Distance, Mistaking it for a Carrion Crow—

unfortunatly We are in bad part of the River for Fish—

NOVEMBER 25, 1820

I spent the whole of this day drawing the *White headed Eagle*, the Weather excidingly warm, the Thermometer rose to 70°, the Wind Blowing Strong a head We remained Still; in the Course of the Afternoon a Small Steam Boat, the *Independance* passed us, I saw with the Spy Glass Old Cap^e Nelson of Louisville; *Butterflies Wasps, & Bees* plenty all day about us =

NOVEMBER 27, 1820

The weather raw and Cloudy, Finished my drawing of the White headed Eagle, having been 4 days at it—

that Noble Bird weighed 8 ½^{lb}, Measured 6 feet 7$^{1/12}$ his Total Length 2^f: 7$^{1/12}$—it proved a Male, the heart extremely Large, My Ball having passed through his Gizzard I could not see any of the Contents =

these Birds are becoming very Numerous, hunt in paires, and roost on the Tall trees above their Nests—One this Morning took up the head of a Wild Goose thrown over board, with as Much ease as a Man Could with the hand—they chase Ducks and if they force one from the Flock he is undoutedly taken, Carried on a Sand Bank and eat by Both Eagles—they are more Shy in the afternoon than in the morning—they seldom Sail High at this season, Watch from the Tops of trees and Dash at any thing that comes near them—to secure a Goose, the Male & femelle, Dive alternatively after it and give it so little time to breath that the poor fellow is forced in a few Minutes—

We are all unwell having eat too freely of the Buck   Mr Shaw went off this Morning to Mr Lovelace's Boat—Made a good run—saw a Large Flock of White Gulls—but Not a Land Bird—Much to My Surprise I have Not Yet seen a Pelican, Nor a Swan on the Barrs or in the River = Malards are the only Ducks We now see—No Game, to be procured Not able to hunt on the Shores—We are Landed at the foot of Flour Island, opposite the first Chicasaw Bluff—the First High Ground since the Chalk banks—

FEBRUARY 19, 1821

the Weather beautifull, Clear & Warm, the Wind having blown hard from the Southwest for 2 days & Nights—

saw this Morning Three Immense Flocks of *Bank Swallows* that past over Me with the rapidity of a Storm, going Northeast, their Cry was heard distinctly, and I knew them first by the Noise they made in the air coming from behind me; the falling of their Dung resembled a heavy but thinly falling Snow; No appearance of any feeding while in our Sight—Which Lasted but a few Minutes—

I was much pleased to see these arbingers of Spring but Where could they be moving So rapidly at this early Season I am quite at a Loss to think, & yet their Passage here was about as long after the Purple Martin that Went By on the 9th Instant as is their Arrival in Kentucky a Month hence—perhaps Were they forced by the east Winds and now Enticed to proceed by the Mildness of the Weather the Thermometer being at 68°—

how far More south must I go Next January & February to see these Millions of Swallows Spending their Winter as Thousands of Warblers, fly Catchers, Thrushes and Myriads of Ducks, Geese, Snipes &^c Do here?—

the Market is regularly furnished with the *English Snipe* Which the french Call^d *Cache cache*, Robins Blue Wing^d Teals Common Teals, Spoon Bill Ducks, Malards, Snow Geese, Canada Geese, Many Cormorants, Coots, Watter Hens, Tell Tale Godwits, Call^d here *Clou Clou* Yellow Shank Snipes, some Sand Hills Cranes, Strings of Blew Warblers, Cardinal Grosbeaks, Common Turtle Doves, Golden Wing^d Wood Peckers &^c.

February 21, 1821

Saw Many Green Baked White Belied Swallows to day and Also some *Martins* Hirundo Purpurea—All of them very Lively and not exibiting much of the Muddy Appearance that immersion in the Swamps about this City would undoubtedly give them had they remained buried in it since Last December at Which time late in that Month they were plenty and remarked Passing by arriving from North & East moving South Westwardly = here they Must Make a Long Pause or Move Eastwardly very Slowly as Seldom do they arrive in Pennsylvania before the 25 of *March* and more frequently in the first days of *April*—they find now here an aboundance of Insects, and the Millions of Musquitoes that raise from the Swamps would Sufice to feed the Swallows of all the World =

saw Many Brown Larks,—

the Fish Crows are remarkably found of alighting in flocks on some Pacan trees about 12 Mile below this City about 9 o'clock in the Morning when they retire On these to rest from their Fishing excursions and remain Croaking untill the Midle of the day—

February 24, 1821

This Morning the Market was well Stocked with Green Backed Swallows *Hirundo Veridis*, the Whole very fat and in beautifull plumage; if these Dear Litle Cherubs have preserved their coats and there flesh so fresh during the pretended Torpor Occasioned by Winter's frost how much more fortunate they are than the Pork Beef & Butter of Kentucky that sowers however well Salted.

I have been assured by Men on whom I can rely that some Winters are so Mild that Swallows are seen from time to time during every Months =

the Swallows in Markets were caught in the holes about houses their resorting places during the Nights—this Morning the Weather is quite Cold, and Yet the Swallows are flying about the Streets, over the River &ᶜ twitering very Lively =

FEBRUARY 25, 1821

Killed Some Green backed White bellied Swallows Hirundo Veridis—extremely fat, the Gizards completely filled with the remains of Winged Insects,—could not perceive any outward diference betwen the sexes,—the femelles however were well Stored with eggs and the Males strongly marked—the Brother of Mʳ Pamar killed a Beautifull White Robin, but his Dog Mangled it so much that I did not draw it—this extraordinary change of Color appeared as the Cause of Old Age, the Bill of the Bird much worn and the Legs were cicatrised in Several parts, the Bird however was very fat, as well as nearly all the others he killed this Day =

saw a few Partridges   these Birds are here much Sought and hunted down without Mercy, not even do the Sportsmen permit a few Paires to remain untouch & thereby the race is nearly extinguished Near the City = We Waded to day through an extensive Swamp with hopes of Meeting Some new Species, but Saw Nothing of the Kind to my astounishment—

July 29, 1821

I had the pleasure of Meeting with Several Red Cockaded Wood Peckers yesterday during a Walk We took to the Pine Woods and procure[d] Two beautifull Males, both alive, being slightly wounded each in the Wing—the particular & very remarkable cry of this Bird can be heard at a very considerable distance of a Still day, in articulation it resembles that of the Hairy Wood Pecker, but is much more Shrill & *Loud*. the Tall pine trees are its Chosen haunts and seldom does it alight on any other kind of Timber—its Motions are quick, gracefull and easy, it Moves in all directions either on the Trunk or Limbs, Looking often very cunningly under the Loose pieces of bark for Insects: is more Shy than any of its Genus, Watching attentively all our Movements below, they kept allways on the opposite side, peeping carefully at us—The second one Shot did not Loose a Moment to think of its Misfortune, the moment it fell to the ground it Hoped briskly to the Nearest tree, and Would soon have reach its top had I not secured it—it defended itself with courage and so powerfully did it peck at my fingers that I was forced to let him go =

Confined in my Hat on my head, they remained Still and Stubborn, I looked at them several times, when I found them trying to hide their Heads as if ashamed to have lost their liberty—the report of my Gun alarmed them every time I Shot when they both uttered a Plaintive Cry—

through the pain of the wound or the heat felt in my hat one died before We reach[d] M[r] Pirries's house—the Other I put in a Cage,—he imediatly review[d] the Premises hoping about and hunting for a place to Work through, and used his Chisel bill with great adroitness sending the small Chips he cut to the right & left and having made his way to the floor, run to the Wall and Climb[d] up it as easily as if the bark of his favorite Pine had been his foot hold, picking between the Bricks and Swallowing every Insect he found =

remarking often his looking under Craks and the litle Shelves in the rough wall, I drew him in that Position = Sorry I am to have to say that Mr Willson's Drawing could not have been Made from the Bird *fresh killed* or if so it was in very bad order about the head, he having put the Small striek of red feathers of the head imediatly over the Eye, where there is a White Line, the red being placed far back of the ear—and the whole of the wing not at all Marked Like that of the Bird—the sides of the breast is also badly represented, the Lines in Nature are Longitudinal only, and Show more of a body—the appearance of this Bird when on the pine trees Would Make one suppose it to be Black all over and the Red Line is often covered by the Crown feathers in the living Bird = I first Met with this Species a few Miles from Nashville, when on My Way to Philadelphia in 1806, seing them from time to time untill I left the first range of Mountains, Called the Cumberland—of the Nest, or time of Incubation I Cannot speak, I am told that during severe winter they will leave the pine Woods and Approach Plantations—

the Length of Both those I attentively examined Was 8 ½ Inches, Breadth 14 ½—the Gizzard filled with heads of Small Ants and a few Minute Insects—the bird smells Strongly of Pine; as I Hope to be soon able to procure the femelle, I May probably with her portrait give More information—

IVORY-BILLED WOODPECKER (1838)

Picus principalis, Linn.

I HAVE ALWAYS IMAGINED, that in the plumage of the beautiful Ivory-billed Woodpecker, there is something very closely allied to the style of colouring of the great Vandyke. The broad extent of its dark glossy body and tail, the large and well-defined white markings of its wings, neck, and bill, relieved by the rich carmine of the pendent crest of the male, and the brilliant yellow of its eye, have never failed to remind me of some of the boldest and noblest productions of that inimitable artist's pencil. So strongly indeed have these thoughts become ingrafted in my mind, as I gradually obtained a more intimate aquaintance with the Ivory-billed Woodpecker, that whenever I have observed one of these birds flying from one tree to another, I have mentally exclaimed, "There goes a Vandyke!" This notion may seem strange, perhaps ludicrous, to you, good reader, but I relate it as a fact, and whether or not it may be found in accordance with your own ideas, after you have inspected the plate in which is represented this great chieftain of the Woodpecker tribe, is perhaps of little consequence.

The Ivory-billed Woodpecker confines its rambles to a comparatively very small portion of the United States, it never having been observed in the Middle States within the memory of any person now living there. In fact, in no portion of these districts does the nature of the woods appear suitable to its remarkable habits.

Descending the Ohio, we meet with this splendid bird for the first time near the confluence of that beautiful river and the Mississippi; after which, following the windings of the latter, either downwards toward the sea, or upwards in the direction of the Missouri, we frequently observe it. On the Atlantic coast, North Carolina may be taken as the limit of its distribution, although now and then an individual of the species may be accidentally seen in Maryland. To the westward of the Mississippi, it is found in all the dense forests bordering the streams which empty their waters into that majestic river, from the very declivities of the Rocky Mountains. The lower parts of the Carolinas, Georgia, Allabama, Louisiana, and Mississippi, are, however, the most favourite resorts of this bird, and in those States it constantly resides, breeds, and passes a life of peaceful enjoyment, finding a profusion of food in all the deep, dark, and gloomy swamps dispersed throughout them.

I wish, kind reader, it were in my power to present to your mind's eye the favourite resort of the Ivory-billed Woodpecker. Would that I could describe the extent of those deep morasses, overshadowed by millions of gigantic dark cypresses, spreading their sturdy moss-covered branches, as if to admonish intruding man to pause and reflect on the many difficulties which he must encounter, should he persist in venturing farther into their almost inaccessible recesses, extending for miles before him, where he should be interrupted by huge projecting branches, here and there the massy trunk of a fallen and decaying tree, and thousands of creeping and twining plants of numberless species! Would that I could represent to you the dangerous nature of the ground, its oozing, spongy, and miry disposition, although covered with a beautiful but treacherous carpeting, composed of the richest mosses, flags, and water-lilies, no sooner receiving the pressure of the foot than it yields and endangers the very life of the adventurer, whilst here and there, as he approaches an opening, that proves merely a lake of black muddy water, his ear is assailed by the dismal croaking of innumerable frogs, the hissing of serpents, or the bellowing of alligators! Would that I could give you an idea of the sultry pestiferous atmosphere that nearly suffocates the intruder during the meridian heat of our dogdays, in those gloomy and horrible swamps! But the attempt to picture these scenes would be vain. Nothing short of ocular demonstration can impress any adequate idea of them.

How often, kind reader, have I thought of the difference of the tasks imposed on different minds, when, travelling in countries far distant from those where birds of this species and others as difficult to be procured are now and then offered for sale in the form of dried skins, I have heard the amateur or closet-naturalist express his astonishment that half-a-crown was asked by the person who had perhaps followed the bird when alive over miles of such swamps, and after procuring it, had prepared its skin in the best manner, and carried it to a market thousands of miles distant from the spot where he had obtained it. I must say, that it has at least grieved me as much as when I have heard some idle fop complain of the poverty of the Gallery of the Louvre, where he had paid nothing, or when I have listened to the same infatuated idler lamenting the loss of his shilling, as he sauntered through the Exhibition Rooms of the Royal Academy of London, or any equally valuable repository of art. But, let us return to the biography of the famed Ivory-billed Woodpecker.

The flight of this bird is graceful in the extreme, although seldom prolonged to more than a few hundred yards at a time, unless when it has to cross a large river, which it does in deep undulations, opening its wings at first to their full extent, and nearly closing them to renew the propelling impulse. The transit from one tree to another, even should the distance be as much as a hundred yards, is performed by a single sweep, and the bird appears as if merely swinging itself from the top of the one tree to that of the other, forming an elegantly curved line. At this moment all the beauty of the plumage is exhibited, and strikes the beholder with pleasure. It never utters any sound whilst on wing, unless during the love season; but at all other times, no sooner has this bird alighted than its remarkable voice is heard, at almost every leap which it makes, whilst ascending against the upper parts of the trunk of a tree, or its highest branches. Its notes are clear, loud, and yet rather plaintive. They are heard at a considerable distance, perhaps half a mile, and resemble the false high note of a clarionet. They are usually repeated three times in succession, and may be represented by the monosyllable *pait, pait, pait.* These are heard so frequently as to induce me to say that the bird spends few minutes of the day without uttering them, and this circumstance leads to its destruction, which is aimed at, not because (as is supposed by some) this species is a destroyer of trees, but more because it is a beautiful bird, and its rich scalp attached to the upper mandible forms an ornament for the war-dress of most of our Indians, or for the shot-pouch of our squatters and hunters, by all of whom the bird is shot merely for that purpose.

Travellers of all nations are also fond of possessing the upper part of the head and the bill of the male, and I have frequently remarked, that on a steam-boat's reaching what we call a *wooding-place,* the *strangers* were very apt to pay a quarter of a dollar for two or three heads of this Woodpecker. I have seen entire belts of Indian chiefs closely ornamented with the tufts and bills of this species, and have observed that a great value is frequently put upon them.

The Ivory-billed Woodpecker nestles earlier in spring than any other species of its tribe. I have observed it boring a hole for that purpose in the beginning of March. The hole is, I believe, always made in the trunk of a live tree, generally an ash or a hagberry, and is at a great height. The birds pay great regard to the particular situation of the tree, and the inclination of its trunk; first, because they prefer retirement, and again, because they are anxious to secure the aperture against the access of water during beating rains. To prevent such a calamity, the hole is generally dug immediately under the junction of a large branch with the trunk. It is first bored horizontally for a few inches, then directly downwards, and not in a spiral manner, as some people have imagined. According to circumstances, this cavity is more or less deep, being sometimes not more than ten inches, whilst at other times it reaches nearly three feet downwards into the core of the tree. I have been led to think that these differences result from the more or less immediate necessity under which the female may be of depositing her eggs, and again have thought that the older the Woodpecker is, the deeper does it make its hole. The average diameter of the different nests which I have examined was about seven inches within, although the entrance, which is perfectly round, is only just large enough to admit the bird.

Both birds work most assiduously at this excavation, one waiting outside to encourage the other, whilst it is engaged in digging, and when the latter is fatigued, taking its place. I have approached trees whilst these Woodpeckers were thus busily employed in forming their nest, and by resting my head against the bark, could easily distinguish every blow given by the bird. I observed that in two instances, when the Woodpeckers saw me thus at the foot of the tree in which they were digging their nest, they abandoned it for ever. For the first brood there are generally six eggs. They are deposited on a few chips at the bottom of the hole, and are of a pure white colour. The young are seen creeping out of the hole about a fortnight before they venture to fly to any other tree. The second brood makes its appearance about the 15th of August.

In Kentucky and Indiana, the Ivory-bills seldom raise more than one brood in the season. The young are at first of the colour of the female, only that they want the crest, which, however, grows rapidly, and towards autumn, particularly in birds of the first breed, is nearly equal to that of the mother. The males have then a slight line of red on the head, and do not attain their richness of plumage until spring, or their full size until the second year. Indeed, even then, a difference is easily observed between them and individuals which are much older.

The food of this species consists principally of beetles, larvæ, and large grubs. No sooner, however, are the grapes of our forests ripe than they are eaten by the Ivory-billed Woodpecker with great avidity. I have seen this bird hang by its claws to the vines, in the position so often assumed by a Titmouse, and, reaching downwards, help itself to a bunch of grapes with much apparent pleasure. Persimons are also sought for by them, as soon as the fruit becomes quite mellow, as are hagberries.

The Ivory-bill is never seen attacking the corn, or the fruit of the orchards, although it is sometimes observed working upon and chipping off the bark from the belted trees of the newly-cleared plantations. It seldom comes near the ground, but prefers at all times the tops of the tallest trees. Should it, however, discover the half-standing broken shaft of a large dead and rotten tree, it attacks it in such a manner as nearly to demolish it in the course of a few days. I have seen the remains of some of these ancient monarchs of our forests so excavated, and that so singularly, that the tottering fragments of the trunk appeared to be merely supported by the great pile of chips by which its base was surrounded. The strength of this Woodpecker is such, that I have seen it detach pieces of bark seven or eight inches in length at a single blow of its powerful bill, and by beginning at the top branch of a dead tree, tear off the bark, to an extent of twenty or thirty feet, in the course of a few hours, leaping downwards with its body in an upward position, tossing its head to the right and left, or leaning it against the bark to ascertain the precise spot where the grubs were concealed, and immediately after renewing its blows with fresh vigour, all the while sounding its loud notes, as if highly delighted.

This species generally moves in pairs, after the young have left their parents. The female is always the most clamorous and the least shy. Their mutual attachment is, I believe, continued through life. Excepting when digging a hole for the reception of their eggs, these birds seldom, if ever, attack living trees, for any other purpose than that of procuring food, in doing which they destroy the insects that would otherwise prove injurious to the trees.

I have frequently observed the male and female retire to rest for the night, into the same hole in which they had long before reared their young. This generally happens a short time after sunset.

When wounded and brought to the ground, the Ivory-bill immediately makes for the nearest tree, and ascends it with great rapidity and perseverance, until it reaches the top branches, when it squats and hides, generally with great effect. Whilst ascending, it moves spirally round the tree, utters its loud *pait, pait, pait*, at almost every hop, but becomes silent the moment it reaches a place where it conceives itself secure. They sometimes cling to the bark with their claws so firmly, as to remain cramped to the spot for several hours after death. When taken by the hand, which is rather a hazardous undertaking, they strike with great violence, and inflict very severe wounds with their bill as well as claws, which are extremely sharp and strong. On such occasions, this bird utters a mournful and very piteous cry.

William Cullen Bryant

TO A WATERFOWL (1821)

Whither, 'midst falling dew,
While glow the heavens with the last steps of day
Far, through their rosy depths, dost thou pursue
    Thy solitary way?

Vainly the fowler's eye
Might mark thy distant flight to do thee wrong,
As, darkly painted on the crimson sky,
    Thy figure floats along.

Seek'st thou the plashy brink
Of weedy lake, or marge of river wide,
Or where the rocking billows rise and sink
    On the chafed ocean side?

There is a Power whose care
Teaches thy way along that pathless coast,—
The desert and illimitable air,—
    Lone wandering, but not lost.

All day thy wings have fanned,
At that far height, the cold thin atmosphere,
Yet stoop not, weary, to the welcome land,
    Though the dark night is near.

And soon that toil shall end,
Soon shalt thou find a summer home, and rest,
And scream among thy fellows; reeds shall bend,
    Soon, o'er thy sheltered nest.

Thou'rt gone, the abyss of heaven
Hath swallow'd up thy form; yet, on my heart
Deeply hath sunk the lesson thou hast given,
    And shall not soon depart.

He, who, from zone to zone,
Guides through the boundless sky thy certain flight,
In the long way that I must tread alone,
    Will lead my steps aright.

Ralph Waldo Emerson

FROM *JOURNALS*, 1838–1862

APRIL 26, 1838

Yesterday P.M. I went to the Cliff with Henry Thoreau. Warm, pleasant, misty weather which the great mountain amphitheatre seemed to drink in with gladness. A crow's voice filled all the miles of air with sound. A bird's voice, even a piping frog enlivens a solitude & makes world enough for us. At night I went out into the dark & saw a glimmering star & heard a frog & Nature seemed to say Well do not these suffice? Here is a new scene, a new experience. Ponder it, Emerson, & not like the foolish world hanker after thunders & multitudes & vast landscapes, the sea or Niagara.

MAY 21, 1856

Yesterday to the Sawmill Brook with Henry. He was in search of yellow violet (pubescens) and menyanthes which he waded into the water for, & which he concluded, on examination, had been out five days. Having found his flowers, he drew out of his breast pocket his diary & read the names of all the plants that should bloom on this day, 20 May; whereof he keeps account as a banker when his notes fall due. rubus triflora, guerens, vaccinium, &c. The cypropedium not due 'till tomorrow. Then we diverged to the brook, where was viburnum dentatum, arrowhead. But his attention was drawn to the redstart which flew about with its *cheah cheah chevet*, & presently to two fine grosbeaks, rosebreasted, whose brilliant scarlet "made the rash gazer wipe his eye," & which he brought nearer with his spy glass, & whose fine clear note he compares to that of a "tanager who has got rid of his hoarseness," then he heard a note which he calls that of the nightwarbler, a bird he has never identified, has been in search of for twelve years; which, always, when he sees, is in the act of diving down into a tree or bush, & which 'tis vain to seek; the only bird that sings indifferently by night & by day. I told him, he must beware of finding & booking him, lest life should have nothing more to show him. He said, "What you seek in vain for half your life, one day you come full upon all the family at dinner.—You seek him like a dream, and as soon as you find him, you become his prey."

June 2, 1856

The finest day the high noon of the year, went with Thoreau in a wagon to Perez Blood's auction; found the myrica flowering; it had already begun to shed its pollen one day, the lowest flowers being effete; found the English hawthorn on Mrs Ripley's hill, ready to bloom; went up the Asabet, & found the *Azalea Nudicaulis* in full bloom, a beautiful show, the *viola muhlenbergi*, the *ranunculus recurvatus*; saw *swamp white oak*, (chestnut-like leaves) *white maple, red maple,*—no *chestnut oak* on the river— Henry told his story of the *Ephemera*, the manna of the fishes, which falls like a snow storm one day in the year, only on this river, not on the Concord, high up in the air as he can see, & blundering down to the river,—(the shad-fly,) the true angler's fly; the fish die of repletion when it comes, the kingfishers wait for their prey. Around us the pepeepee of the king bird kind was noisy.

MAY 30, 1857

Walk this PM with Henry T. Found the *perfoliate uvularia* for the first time in Lincoln by Flint's Pond, found the *chestnut sided warbler*, which, I doubt not, I have seen already, & mistaken for the *particolored*. Heard the note of the latter, which resembles a locust-sound. Saw the cuckoo.

MARCH 3, 1862

The snow still lies even with the tops of the walls across the Walden road, and, this afternoon, I waded through the woods to my grove. A chicadee came out to greet me, flew about within reach of my hands, perched on the nearest bough, flew down into the snow, rested there two seconds, then up again, just over my head, & busied himself on the dead bark. I whistled to him through my teeth, and, (I think, in response,) he began at once to whistle. I promised him crumbs, & must not go again to these woods without them. I suppose the best food to carry would be the meat of shagbarks or castille nuts. Thoreau tells me that they are very sociable with wood-choppers, & will take crumbs from their hands.

Henry David Thoreau

FROM *JOURNALS*, 1852–1858

MARCH 10, 1852

I was reminded, this morning before I rose, of those undescribed ambrosial mornings of summer which I can remember, when a thousand birds were heard gently twittering and ushering in the light, like the argument to a new canto of an epic and heroic poem. The serenity, the infinite promise, of such a morning! The song or twitter of birds drips from the leaves like dew. Then there was something divine and immortal in our life. When I have waked up on my couch in the woods and seen the day dawning, and heard the twittering of the birds.

I see flocks of a dozen bluebirds together. The warble of this bird is innocent and celestial, like its color. Saw a sparrow, perhaps a song sparrow, flitting amid the young oaks where the ground was covered with snow. I think that this is an indication that the ground is quite bare a little further south. Probably the spring birds never fly far over a snow-clad country. A wood-chopper tells me he heard a robin this morning. I see the reticulated leaves of the rattlesnake-plantain in the woods, quite fresh and green. What is the little chickweed-like plant already springing up on the top of the Cliffs? There are some other plants with bright-green leaves which have either started somewhat or have never suffered from the cold under the snow. Summer clenches hands with summer under the snow. I am pretty sure that I heard the chuckle of a ground squirrel among the warm and bare rocks of the Cliffs. The earth is perhaps two thirds bare to-day. The mosses are now very handsome, like young grass pushing up. Heard the phœbe note of the chickadee to-day for the first time. I had at first heard their *day-day-day* ungratefully,—ah! you but carry my thoughts back to winter,—but anon I found that they too had become spring birds; they had changed their note. Even they feel the influence of spring.

April 19, 1852

That last flock of geese yesterday is still in my eye. After hearing their clangor, looking southwest, we saw them just appearing over a dark pine wood, in an irregular waved line, one abreast of the other, as it were breasting the air and pushing it before them. It made you think of the streams of Cayster, etc., etc. They carry weight, such a weight of metal in the air. Their dark waved outline as they disappear. The grenadiers of the air. Man pygmifies himself at sight of these inhabitants of the air. These stormy days they do not love to fly; they alight in some retired marsh or river. From their lofty pathway they can easily spy out the most extensive and retired swamp. How many there must be, that one or more flocks are seen to go over almost every farm in New England in the spring.

Scared up three blue herons in the little pond close by, quite near us. It was a grand sight to see them rise, so slow and stately, so long and limber, with an undulating motion from head to foot, undulating also their large wings, undulating in two directions, and looking warily about them. With this graceful, limber, undulating motion  they arose, as if so they got under way, their two legs trailing parallel far behind like an earthy residuum to be left behind. They are large, like birds of Syrian lands, and seemed to oppress the earth, and hush the hillside to silence, as they winged their way over it, looking back toward us. It would affect our thoughts, deepen and perchance darken our reflections, if such huge birds flew in numbers in our sky. Have the effect of magnetic passes. They are few and rare. Among the birds of celebrated flight, storks, cranes, geese, and ducks. The legs hang down like a weight which they raise, to pump up as it were with its wings and convey out of danger.

The mist to-day makes those near distances which Gilpin tells of. I saw, looking from the railroad to Fair Haven Hill soon after we started, four such,—the wood on E. Hubbard's meadow, dark but open; that of Hubbard's Grove, showing the branches of the trees; Potter's pitch pines, perhaps one solid black mass with outline only distinct; Brown's on the Cliff, but dimly seen through the mist,— one above and beyond the other, with vales of mist between.

To see the larger and wilder birds, you must go forth in the great storms like this. At such times they frequent our neighborhood and trust themselves in our midst. A life of fair-weather walks *might* never show you the goose sailing on our waters, or the great heron feeding here. When the storm increases, then these great birds that carry the mail of the seasons lay to. To see wild life you must go forth at a wild season. When it rains and blows, keeping men indoors, then the lover of Nature must forth. Then returns Nature to her wild estate. In pleasant sunny weather you may catch butterflies, but only when the storm rages that lays prostrate the forest and wrecks the mariner, do you come upon the feeding-grounds of wildest fowl,— of heron and geese.

MAY 7, 1852

Has been a dew, which wets the feet, and I see a very thin fog over the low ground, the first fog, which must be owing to the warm weather. Heard a robin singing powerfully an hour ago, and song sparrows, and the cocks. No peeping frogs in the morning, or rarely.

The toads sing(?), but not as at evening. I walk half a mile (to Hubbard's Pool, in the road), before I reach those I heard,—only two or three. The sound is uttered so low and over water; still it is wonderful that it should be heard so far. The traveller rarely perceives when he comes near the source of it, nor when he is farthest away from it. Like the will-o'-the-wisp, it will lead one a long chase over the fields and meadows to find one. They dream more or less at all hours now. I see the relation to the frogs in the throat of many a man. The full throat has relation to the distended paunch.

I would fain see the sun as a moon, more weird. The sun now rises in a rosaceous amber. Methinks the birds sing more some mornings than others, when I cannot see the reason. I smell the damp path, and derive vigor from the earthy scent between Potter's and Hayden's. Beginning, I may say, with robins, song sparrows, chip-birds, bluebirds, etc., I walked through larks, pewees, pigeon woodpeckers, chickadee *tull-a-lulls*, to towhees, huckleberry-birds, wood thrushes, brown thrasher, jay, catbird, etc., etc. Entered a cool stratum of air beyond Hayden's after the warmth of yesterday. The *Viola pedata* still in bud only, and the other (*q. v.*) Hear the first partridge drum. The first oven-bird. A wood thrush which I thought a dozen rods off, was only two or three, to my surprise, and betrayed himself by moving, like a large sparrow with ruffled feathers, and quirking his tail like a pewee, on a low branch. Blackbirds are seen going over the woods with a chattering bound to some meadow.

A rich bluish mist now divides the vales in the eastern horizon mile after mile. (I am ascending Fair Haven.) An oval-leaved pyrola (evergreen) in Brown's pines on Fair Haven.

Cliffs.—This is the gray morning; the sun risen; a very thin mist on the landscape; the falling water smooth. Far below, a screaming jay seen flying, against the bare stems of the pines. The young oaks on the plain, the pines standing here and there, the walls in Conantum pastures seen in the sun, the little groves on the opposite side of the river lit up by it while I am in shade, these are memorable and belong to the hour.

Here at this hour the brown thrasher often drowns the other birds. The towhee has been a main bird for regular morning singing in the woods for a little while. The creeper is regularly heard, too. Found the first strawberry blossoms (*Fragaria Virginiana*) on Fair Haven. The sedge grass blossom is now quite large and showy on the dry hillside where the wood has recently been cut off.

I think that birds vary their notes considerably with the seasons. When I hear a bird singing, I cannot think of any words that will imitate it. What word can stand in place of a bird's note? You would have to hurry it, or surround it with a *chevaux de frise* of accents, and exhaust the art of the musical composer besides with your different bars, to represent it, and finally get a bird to sing it, to perform it. It has so little relation to words. The wood thrush says *ah-tully-tully* for one strain. There appear to be one or more little warblers in the woods this morning which are new to the season, about which I am in doubt, myrtle-birds among them. For now, before the leaves, they begin to people the trees in this warm weather. The first wave of summer from the south. The purple finch (sober-colored) is a rich singer. As I said the other day, something like the warbling vireo, only louder, clearer, mellower, and more various. Bank swallows at Hayden's.

The vireo comes with warm weather, midwife to the leaves of the elms. I see little ant-hills in the path, already raised. How long have they been? The first small pewee sings now *che-vet*, or rather chirrups *chevet*, *tche-vet*—a rather delicate bird with a large head and two white bars on wings. The first summer yellowbirds on the willow causeway. The birds I have lately mentioned come not singly, as the earliest, but all at once, *i. e.* many yellowbirds all over town. Now I remember the yellowbird comes when the willows begin to leave out. (And the small pewee on the willows also.) So yellow. They bring summer with them and the sun, *tche-tche-tche-tcha tcha-tchar.* Also they haunt the oaks, white and swamp white, where are not leaves.

July 5, 1852

The robin, the red-eye, the veery, the wood thrush, etc., etc.

The wood thrush's is no opera music; it is not so much the composition as the strain, the tone,—cool bars of melody from the atmosphere of everlasting morning or evening. It is the quality of the song, not the sequence. In the peawai's note there is some sultriness, but in the thrush's, though heard at noon, there is the liquid coolness of things that are just drawn from the bottom of springs. The thrush alone declares the immortal wealth and vigor that is in the forest. Here is a bird in whose strain the story is told, though Nature waited for the science of æsthetics to discover it to man. Whenever a man hears it, he is young, and Nature is in her spring. Wherever he hears it, it is a new world and a free country, and the gates of heaven are not shut against him. Most other birds sing from the level of my ordinary cheerful hours—a carol; but this bird never fails to speak to me out of an ether purer than that I breathe, of immortal beauty and vigor. He deepens the significance of all things seen in the light of his strain. He sings to make men take higher and truer views of things. He sings to amend their institutions; to relieve the slave on the plantation and the prisoner in his dungeon, the slave in the house of luxury and the prisoner of his own low thoughts.

June 7, 1853

Going through Thrush Alley, see the froth on the base of the shoots of the pitch pine, now three or four to ten inches long.

Visited my nighthawk on her nest. Could hardly believe my eyes when I stood within seven feet and beheld her sitting on her eggs, her head to me. She looked so Saturnian, so one with the earth, so sphinx-like, a relic of the reign of Saturn which Jupiter did not destroy, a riddle that might well cause a man to go dash his head against a stone. It was not an actual living creature, far less a winged creature of the air, but a figure in stone or bronze, a fanciful production of art, like the gryphon or phœnix. In fact, with its breast toward me, and owing to its color or size no bill perceptible, it looked like the end of a brand, such as are common in a clearing, its breast mottled or alternately waved with dark brown and gray, its flat, grayish, weather-beaten crown, its eyes nearly closed, purposely, lest those bright beads should betray it, with the stony cunning of the sphinx. A fanciful work in bronze to ornament a mantel. It was enough to fill one with awe. The sight of this creature sitting on its eggs impressed me with the venerableness of the globe. There was nothing novel about it. All the while, this seemingly sleeping bronze sphinx, as motionless as the earth, was watching me with intense anxiety through those narrow slits in its eyelids. Another step, and it fluttered down the hill close to the ground, with a wobbling motion, as if touching the ground now with the tip of one wing, now with the other, so ten rods to the water, which it skimmed close over a few rods, then rose and soared in the air above me. Wonderful creature, which sits motionless on its eggs on the barest, most exposed hills, through pelting storms of rain or hail, as if it were a rock or a part of the earth itself, the outside of the globe, with its eyes shut and its wings folded, and, after the two days' storm, when you think it has become a fit symbol of the rheumatism, it suddenly rises into the air a bird, one of the most aerial, supple, and graceful of creatures, without stiffness in its wings or joints! It was a fit prelude to meeting Prometheus bound to his rock on Caucasus.

JUNE 8, 1853

As I stood by this pond, I heard a hawk scream, and, looking up, saw a pretty large one circling not far off and incessantly screaming, as I at first supposed to scare and so discover its prey, but its screaming was so incessant and it circled from time to time so near me, as I moved southward, that I began to think it had a nest near by and was angry at my intrusion into its domains. As I moved, the bird still followed and screamed, coming sometimes quite near or within gunshot, then circling far off or high into the sky. At length, as I was looking up at it, thinking it the only living creature within view, I was singularly startled to behold, as my eye by chance penetrated deeper into the blue,—the abyss of blue above, which I had taken for a solitude,—its mate silently soaring at an immense height and seemingly indifferent to me. We are surprised to discover that there can be an eye on us on that side, and so little suspected, that the heavens are full of eyes, though they look so blue and spotless. Then I knew it was the female that circled and screamed below. At last the latter rose gradually to meet her mate, and they circled together there, as if they could not possibly feel any anxiety on my account. When I drew nearer to the tall trees where I suspected the nest to be, the female descended again, swept by screaming still nearer to me just over the tree-tops, and finally, while I was looking for the orchis in the swamp, alighted on a white pine twenty or thirty rods off. (The great fringed orchis just open.) At length I detected the nest about eighty feet from the ground, in a very large white pine by the edge of the swamp. It was about three feet in diameter, of dry sticks, and a young hawk, apparently as big as its mother, stood on the edge of the nest looking down at me, and only moving its head when I moved. In its imperfect plumage and by the slow motion of its head it reminded me strongly of a vulture, so large and gaunt. It appeared a tawny brown on its neck and breast, and dark brown or blackish on wings. The mother was light beneath, and apparently lighter still on rump.

APRIL 23, 1854

As for the birds, I have this to remark: The crows still frequent the meadows. The lark sings morning and evening. The blackbirds— red-wing and crow—have since their arrival kept up their *bobylee* and chattering and split notes on the willows and maples by the river and along the meadow's edge. They appear to depend much (as well as crows and robins) on the meadow, just left bare, for their food. They are the noisiest birds yet. Both still fly in flocks, though the male red-wings have *begun* to chase the females. Robins still frequent the meadows in flocks and sing in the rain. The song sparrows not in such flocks nor singing so tumultuously along the watercourses in the morning as in the last half of March. How wary they are! They will dodge you for half an hour behind a wall or a twig, and only a stone will make them start, looking every which way in a minute. So the blackbirds, both kinds, sidle till they bring a twig between me and them. The flock of black ducks which stayed by so long is now reduced to a quarter part their number. Before the 4th or 5th of April the *F. hyemalis* was apparently the most abundant bird of any, in great drifting flocks with their lively jingle, their light-colored bill against slate breasts; then, on the advent of warmer weather, the greater part departed. Have the fox sparrows gone also? I have not seen them of late. As for hawks, after the one or two larger (perhaps) hen-hawks in the winter and a smaller one in December (?), the first were *large* marsh (?) hawks on trees on the meadow edge or skimming along it; since which the eagle, the sharp-shinned, and the smaller brown and white-rumped over meadows, which may be the same, etc., etc. Have seen the black duck, golden-eye, merganser, blue(?)-winged teal, wood duck. The golden-eye seems to have gone. Heard a nuthatch yesterday, April 22d. The tree sparrows are the prevailing bird on ground, and most numerous of any for the past month except one while the hyemalis. They are a chubby little bird with a clear chestnut crown, a dark spot on the otherwise clear whitish breast, and two light bars on the wings. The pigeon woodpecker now scolds long and loud morning and evening. The snipes are still feeding on the meadows. The turtle dove darts solitary about as if lost, or it had lost its mate. The yellow redpoll, with a faint clear *chip*, is the commonest *yellow* bird on hills, etc., about water. The chip sparrow does not sing much in morning yet. New kinds of warblers have begun to come within a few days.

The myrtle-bird,—yellow-rumped warbler,—was not this warbler *c* of the 20th?—on the willows, alders, and the wall by Hubbard's Bridge, slate and white spotted with yellow. Its note is a *fine*, rapid, somewhat hissing or whistling *se se se se se ser riddler se*, somewhat like the common yellowbird's. The yellow redpolls are very common on the willows and alders and in the road near the bridge. They keep jerking their tails. I heard one male sing a jingle like *che ve ve ve ve vē*, very fast, and accenting the last syllable. They are quite tame. I sit awhile on the lee side of Conant's Wood, in the sun, amid the dry oak leaves, and hear from time to time the *fine* ringing note of a pine warbler, which I do not see. It reminds me of former days and indescribable things.

Saw my white-headed eagle again, first at the same place, the outlet of Fair Haven Pond.—It was a fine sight, he is mainly—*i. e.* his wings and body—so black against the sky, and they contrast so strongly with his white head and tail. He was first flying low over the water; then rose gradually and circled westward toward White Pond. Lying on the ground with my glass, I could watch him very easily, and by turns he gave me all possible views of himself. When I observed him edgewise I noticed that the tips of his wings curved upward slightly the more, like a stereotyped undulation. He rose very high at last, till I almost lost him in the clouds, circling or rather *looping* along westward, high over river and wood

and farm, effectually concealed in the sky. We who live this plodding life here below never know how many eagles fly over us. They are concealed in the empyrean. I think I have got the worth of my glass now that it has revealed to me the white-headed eagle. Now I see him edgewise like a black ripple in the air, his white head still as ever turned to earth, and now he turns his under side to me, and I behold the full breadth of his broad black wings, somewhat ragged at the edges. I had first seen two white ducks far off just above the outlet of the pond, mistaking them for the foaming crest of a wave. These flew soon, perhaps scared by the eagle. I think they were a male and female red-breasted merganser (though I did not see the red of the breast), for I saw his *red bill*, and his head was not large with a crest like the golden-eye; very white on breast and sides, the female browner. As ducks often do, they first flew directly and unhesitatingly up the stream, low over the water, for half a mile, then turned and came down, flying thirty or forty feet above the water, the male leading till they were out of sight. This is the way with them, I notice; they first fly in one direction and then go off to alight in another. When they came down the river, the male leading, they were a very good example of the peculiar flight of ducks. They appeared perfectly in a line one behind the other. When they are not they preserve perfect parallelism. This is because of their long necks and feet,—the wings appearing to be attached midway,—and moreover, in this case, of their perfectly level flight, as if learned from skimming over the water. Directly after rose two blue herons from the meadow.

MAY 7, 1855

A short distance beyond this and the hawk's-nest pine, I observed a middling-sized red oak standing a little aslant on the side-hill over the swamp, with a pretty large hole in one side about fifteen feet from the ground, where apparently a limb on which a felled tree lodged had been cut some years before and so broke out a cavity. I thought that such a hole was too good a one not to be improved by some inhabitant of the wood. Perhaps the gray squirrels I had just seen had their nest there. Or was not the entrance big enough to admit a screech owl? So I thought I would tap on it and put my ear to the trunk and see if I could hear anything stirring within it, but I heard nothing. Then I concluded to look into it. So I shinned up, and when I reached up one hand to the hole to pull myself up by it, the thought passed through my mind perhaps something may take hold my fingers, but nothing did. The first limb was nearly opposite to the hole, and, resting on this, I looked in, and, to my great surprise, there squatted, filling the hole, which was about six inches deep and five to six wide, a salmon-brown bird not so big as a partridge, seemingly asleep within three inches of the top and close to my face. It was a minute or two before I made it out to be an owl. It was a salmon-brown or fawn (?) above, the feathers shafted with small blackish-brown somewhat hastate (?) marks, *grayish* toward the ends of the wings and tail, as far as I could see. A large white circular space about or behind eye, banded in rear by a pretty broad (one third of an inch) and quite conspicuous perpendicular *dark*-brown stripe. Egret, say one and a quarter inches long, sharp, triangular, reddish-brown without mainly. It lay crowded in that small space, with its tail somewhat bent up and one side of its head turned up with one egret, and its large dark eye open only by a long slit about a sixteenth of an inch wide; visible breathing. After a little while I put in one hand and stroked it repeatedly, whereupon it reclined its head a little lower and closed its eye entirely. Though curious to know what was under it, I disturbed it no farther at that time.

Returning by owl's nest, about one hour before sunset, I climbed up and looked in again. The owl was gone, but there were four nearly round *dirty brownish white* eggs, quite warm, on nothing but the bits of rotten wood which made the bottom of the hole. The eggs were very nearly as large at one end as the other, slightly oblong, 1 ⅜ inches by 1 ⅜, as nearly as I could measure. I took out one. It would probably have hatched within a week, the young being considerably feathered and the bill remarkably developed. Perhaps she heard me coming, and so left the nest. My bird corresponds in color, as far as I saw it, with Wilson's *Strix asio*, but not his *nævia*, which Nuttall and others consider a young (?) bird, though the egg was not pure white. I do not remember that my bird was barred or *mottled* at all.

Nuttall says, Little Screech-Owl: Greenland to Florida; chiefly prey on mice; also small birds, beetles, crickets, etc.; nest in May and June, and lined with etc., etc., eggs four to six; several bluebirds, blackbirds, and song sparrows in one. In cloudy weather come out earlier. Wilson's thrush attacked one. Note in autumn, "hō, hŏ hŏ hŏ hŏ hŏ hŏ, proceeding from high and clear to a low guttural shake or trill."

Was not that an owl's feather which I found half a mile beyond, downy more than half, and with base and separate white *points* beyond a dark band at the end?

Was not mine a bird of last year? But MacGillivray says of owls that the young differ very little from the old; "the older the individual becomes, the more simple is the colouring; the dark markings diminish in extent, and the finer mottlings are gradually obliterated."

MAY 12, 1855

As I approached the owl's nest, I saw her run past the hole up into that part of the hollow above it, and probably she was there when I thought she had flown on the 7th. I looked in, and at first did not know what I saw. One of the three remaining eggs was hatched, and a little downy *white* young one, two or three times as long as an egg, lay helpless between the two remaining eggs. Also a dead white-bellied mouse (*Mus leucopus*) lay with them, its tail curled round one of the eggs. Wilson says of his red owl (*Strix asio*),—with which this apparently corresponds, and not with the mottled, though my egg is not "pure white,"—that "the young are at first covered with a whitish down."

OCTOBER 19, 1856

See quite a flock of myrtle-birds,—which I might carelessly have mistaken for slate-colored snowbirds,—flitting about on the rocky hillside under Conantum Cliff. They show about three white or light-colored spots when they fly, *commonly* no bright yellow, though some are pretty bright. They perch on the side of the dead mulleins, on rocks, on the ground, and directly dart off apparently in pursuit of some insect. I hear no note from them. They are thus near or on the ground, then, not as in spring.

I have often noticed the inquisitiveness of birds, as the other day of a sparrow, whose motions I should not have supposed to have any reference to me, if I had not watched it from first to last. I stood on the edge of a pine and birch wood. It flitted from seven or eight rods distant to a pine within a rod of me, where it hopped about stealthily and chirped awhile, then flew as many rods the other side and hopped about there a spell, then back to the pine again, as near me as it dared, and again to its first position, very restless all the while. Generally I should have supposed that there was more than one bird, or that it was altogether accidental,—that the chipping of this sparrow eight or ten rods away had no reference to me,—for I could see nothing peculiar about it. But when I brought my glass to bear on it, I found that it was almost steadily eying me and was all alive with excitement.

OCTOBER 28, 1857

I look up and see a male marsh hawk with his clean-cut wings, that has just skimmed past above my head,—not at all disturbed, only tilting his body a little, now twenty rods off, with demi-semi-quaver of his wings. He is a very neat flyer. Again, I hear the scream of a hen-hawk, soaring and circling onward. I do not often see the marsh hawk thus. What a regular figure this fellow makes on high, with his broad tail and broad wings! Does he perceive me, that he rises higher and circles to one side? He goes round now one full circle without a flap, tilting his wing a little; then flaps three or four times and rises higher. Now he comes on like a billow, screaming. Steady as a planet in its orbit, with his head bent down, but on second thought that small sprout-land seems worthy of a longer scrutiny, and he gives one circle backward over it. His scream is somewhat like the whinnering of a horse, if it is not rather a *split squeal.* It is a hoarse, tremulous breathing forth of his winged energy. But why is it so regularly repeated at that height? Is it to scare his prey, that he may see by its motion where it is, or to inform its mate or companion of its whereabouts? Now he crosses the at present broad river steadily, deserving to have one or two rabbits at least to swing about him. What majesty there is in this small bird's flight! The hawks are large-souled.

DECEMBER 12, 1858

Crossing the fields west of our Texas house, I see an immense flock of snow buntings, I think the largest that I ever saw. There must be a thousand or two at least. There is but three inches, at most, of crusted and dry frozen snow, and they are running amid the weeds which rise above it. The weeds are chiefly *Juncus tenuis* (?), but its seeds are apparently gone. I find, however, the glumes of the piper grass scattered about where they have been. The flock is at first about equally divided into two parts about twenty rods apart, but birds are incessantly flitting across the interval to join the pioneer flock, until all are united. They are very restless, running amid the weeds and continually changing their ground. They will suddenly rise again a few seconds after they have alighted, as if alarmed, but after a short wheel settle close by. Flying from you, in some positions, you see only or chiefly the black part of their bodies, and then, as they wheel, the white comes into view, contrasted prettily with the former, and in all together at the same time. Seen flying higher against a cloudy sky they look like large snowflakes. When they rise all together their note is like the rattling of nuts in a bag, as if a whole binful were rolled from side to side. They also utter from time to time—*i. e.*, individuals do—a clear rippling note, perhaps of alarm, or a call. It is remarkable that their notes above described should resemble the lesser redpolls! Away goes this great wheeling, rambling flock, rolling through the air, and you cannot easily tell where they will settle. Suddenly the pioneers (or a part not foremost) will change their course when in full career, and when at length they know it, the rushing flock on the other side will be fetched about as it were with an undulating jerk, as in the boys' game of snap-the-whip, and those that occupy the place of the snapper are gradually off after their leaders on the new tack. As far as I observe, they confine themselves to upland, not alighting in the meadows. Like a snow-storm they come rushing down from the north. The extremities of the wings are black, while the parts next their bodies are [not] black. They are unusually abundant now.

Emily Dickinson

A BIRD CAME DOWN THE WALK – (C. 1862)

A Bird came down the Walk –
He did not know I saw –
He bit an Angleworm in halves
And ate the fellow, raw,

And then he drank a Dew
From a convenient Grass –
And then hopped sidewise to the Wall
To let a Beetle pass –

He glanced with rapid eyes
That hurried all around –
They looked like frightened Beads, I thought –
He stirred his Velvet Head

Like one in danger, Cautious,
I offered him a Crumb
And he unrolled his feathers
And rowed him softer home –

Than Oars divide the Ocean,
Too silver for a seam –
Or Butterflies, off Banks of Noon
Leap, plashless as they swim.

THE WAY TO KNOW THE BOBOLINK (C. 1873)

The Way to know the Bobolink
From every other Bird
Precisely as the Joy of him –
Obliged to be inferred.

Of impudent Habiliment
Attired to defy,
Impertinence subordinate
At times to Majesty.

Of Sentiments seditious
Amenable to Law –
As Heresies of Transport
Or Puck's Apostacy.

Extrinsic to Attention
Too intimate with Joy –
He compliments existence
Until allured away

By Seasons or his Children –
Adult and urgent grown –
Or unforeseen aggrandizement
Or, happily, Renown –

By Contrast certifying
The Bird of Birds is gone –
How nullified the Meadow –
Her Sorcerer withdrawn!

Walt Whitman

BIRDS MIGRATING AT MIDNIGHT (1882)

Did you ever chance to hear the midnight flight of birds passing through the air and darkness overhead, in countless armies, changing their early or late summer habitat? It is something not to be forgotten. A friend called me up just after 12 last night to mark the peculiar noise of unusually immense flocks migrating north (rather late this year.) In the silence, shadow and delicious odor of the hour, (the natural perfume belonging to the night alone,) I thought it rare music. You could *hear* the characteristic motion—once or twice "the rush of mighty wings," but oftener a velvety rustle, long drawn out—sometimes quite near—with continual calls and chirps, and some song-notes. It all lasted from 12 till after 3. Once in a while the species was plainly distinguishable; I could make out the bobolink, tanager, Wilson's thrush, white-crown'd sparrow, and occasionally from high in the air came the notes of the plover.

BIRD-WHISTLING (1882)

How much music (wild, simple, savage, doubtless, but so tart-sweet,) there is in mere whistling. It is four-fifths of the utterance of birds. There are all sorts and styles. For the last half-hour, now, while I have been sitting here, some feather'd fellow away off in the bushes has been repeating over and over again what I may call a kind of throbbing whistle. And now a bird about the robin size has just appear'd, all mulberry red, flitting among the bushes—head, wings, body, deep red, not very bright—no song, as I have heard. *4 o'clock*: There is a real concert going on around me—a dozen different birds pitching in with a will. There have been occasional rains, and the growths all show its vivifying influences. As I finish this, seated on a log close by the pond-edge, much chirping and trilling in the distance, and a feather'd recluse in the woods near by is singing deliciously—not many notes, but full of music of almost human sympathy—continuing for a long, long while.

BIRDS—AND A CAUTION (1882)

HOME AGAIN; down temporarily in the Jersey woods. Between 8 and 9 A.M. a full concert of birds, from different quarters, in keeping with the fresh scent, the peace, the naturalness all around me. I am lately noticing the russet-back, size of the robin or a trifle less, light breast and shoulders, with irregular dark stripes—tail long—sits hunch'd up by the hour these days, top of a tall bush, or some tree, singing blithely. I often get near and listen, as he seems tame; I like to watch the working of his bill and throat, the quaint sidle of his body, and flex of his long tail. I hear the woodpecker, and night and early morning the shuttle of the whip-poor-will—noons, the gurgle of thrush delicious, and *meo-o-ow* of the cat-bird. Many I cannot name; but I do not very particularly seek information. (You must not know too much, or be too precise or scientific about birds and trees and flowers and water-craft; a certain free margin, and even vagueness—perhaps ignorance, credulity—helps your enjoyment of these things, and of the sentiment of feather'd, wooded, river, or marine Nature generally. I repeat it—don't want to know too exactly, or the reasons why. My own notes have been written off-hand in the latitude of middle New Jersey. Though they describe what I saw—what appear'd to me—I dare say the expert ornithologist, botanist or entomologist will detect more than one slip in them.)

Sarah Orne Jewett

A WHITE HERON (1886)

I.

THE WOODS were already filled with shadows one June evening, just before eight o'clock, though a bright sunset still glimmered faintly among the trunks of the trees. A little girl was driving home her cow, a plodding, dilatory, provoking creature in her behavior, but a valued companion for all that. They were going away from whatever light there was, and striking deep into the woods, but their feet were familiar with the path, and it was no matter whether their eyes could see it or not.

There was hardly a night the summer through when the old cow could be found waiting at the pasture bars; on the contrary, it was her greatest pleasure to hide herself away among the high huckleberry bushes, and though she wore a loud bell she had made the discovery that if one stood perfectly still it would not ring. So Sylvia had to hunt for her until she found her, and call Co'! Co'! with never an answering Moo, until her childish patience was quite spent. If the creature had not given good milk and plenty of it, the case would have seemed very different to her owners. Besides, Sylvia had all the time there was, and very little use to make of it. Sometimes in pleasant weather it was a consolation to look upon the cow's pranks as an intelligent attempt to play hide and seek, and as the child had no playmates she lent herself to this amusement with a good deal of zest. Though this chase had been so long that the wary animal herself had given an unusual signal of her whereabouts, Sylvia had only laughed when she came upon Mistress Moolly at the swamp-side, and urged her affectionately homeward with a twig of birch leaves. The old cow was not inclined to wander farther, she even turned in the right direction for once as they left the pasture, and stepped along the road at a good pace. She was quite ready to be milked now, and seldom stopped to browse. Sylvia wondered what her grandmother would say because they were so late. It was a great while since she had left home at half-past five o'clock, but everybody knew the difficulty of making this errand a short one. Mrs. Tilley had chased the hornéd torment too many summer evenings herself to blame any one else for lingering, and was only thankful as she waited that she had Sylvia, nowadays, to give such valuable assistance. The good woman suspected that Sylvia loitered occasionally on her own account; there never was such a child for straying about out-of-doors since the world was made! Everybody said that it was a good change for a little maid who had tried to grow for eight years in a crowded manufacturing town, but, as for Sylvia herself, it seemed as if she never had been alive at all before she came to live at the farm. She thought often with wistful compassion of a wretched geranium that belonged to a town neighbor.

"'Afraid of folks,'" old Mrs. Tilley said to herself, with a smile, after she had made the unlikely choice of Sylvia from her daughter's houseful of children, and was returning to the farm. "'Afraid of folks,' they said! I guess she won't be troubled no great with 'em up to the old place!" When they reached the door of the lonely house and stopped to unlock it, and the cat came to purr loudly, and rub against them, a deserted pussy, indeed, but fat with young robins, Sylvia whispered that this was a beautiful place to live in, and she never should wish to go home.

The companions followed the shady wood-road, the cow taking slow steps and the child very fast ones. The cow stopped long at the brook to drink, as if the pasture were not half a swamp, and Sylvia stood still and waited, letting her bare feet cool themselves in the shoal water, while the great twilight moths struck softly against her. She waded on through the brook as the cow moved away, and listened to the thrushes with a heart that beat fast with pleasure. There was a stirring in the great boughs overhead. They were full of little birds and beasts that seemed to be wide awake, and going about their world, or else saying good-night to each other in sleepy twitters. Sylvia herself felt sleepy as she walked along. However, it was not much farther to the house, and the air was soft and sweet. She was not often in the woods so late as this, and it made her feel as if she were a part of the gray shadows and the moving leaves. She was just thinking how long it seemed since she first came to the farm a year ago, and wondering if everything went on in the noisy town just the same as when she was there; the thought of the great red-faced boy who used to chase and frighten her made her hurry along the path to escape from the shadow of the trees.

Suddenly this little woods-girl is horror-stricken to hear a clear whistle not very far away. Not a bird's-whistle, which would have a sort of friendliness, but a boy's whistle, determined, and somewhat aggressive. Sylvia left the cow to whatever sad fate might await her, and stepped discreetly aside into the bushes, but she was just too late. The enemy had discovered her, and called out in a very cheerful and persuasive tone, "Halloa, little girl, how far is it to the road?" and trembling Sylvia answered almost inaudibly, "A good ways."

She did not dare to look boldly at the tall young man, who carried a gun over his shoulder, but she came out of her bush and again followed the cow, while he walked alongside.

"I have been hunting for some birds," the stranger said kindly, "and I have lost my way, and need a friend very much. Don't be afraid," he added gallantly. "Speak up and tell me what your name is, and whether you think I can spend the night at your house, and go out gunning early in the morning."

Sylvia was more alarmed than before. Would not her grandmother consider her much to blame? But who could have foreseen such an accident as this? It did not seem to be her fault, and she hung her head as if the stem of it were broken, but managed to answer "Sylvy," with much effort when her companion again asked her name.

Mrs. Tilley was standing in the doorway when the trio came into view. The cow gave a loud moo by way of explanation.

"Yes, you 'd better speak up for yourself, you old trial! Where 'd she tucked herself away this time, Sylvy?" But Sylvia kept an awed silence; she knew by instinct that her grandmother did not comprehend the gravity of the situation. She must be mistaking the stranger for one of the farmer-lads of the region.

The young man stood his gun beside the door, and dropped a lumpy game-bag beside it; then he bade Mrs. Tilley good-evening, and repeated his wayfarer's story, and asked if he could have a night's lodging.

"Put me anywhere you like," he said. "I must be off early in the morning, before day; but I am very hungry, indeed. You can give me some milk at any rate, that 's plain."

"Dear sakes, yes," responded the hostess, whose long slumbering hospitality seemed to be easily awakened. "You might fare better if you went out to the main road a mile or so, but you 're welcome to what we 've got. I 'll milk right off, and you make yourself at home. You can sleep on husks or feathers," she proffered graciously. "I raised them all myself. There 's good pasturing for geese just below here towards the ma'sh. Now step round and set a plate for the gentleman, Sylvy!" And Sylvia promptly stepped. She was glad to have something to do, and she was hungry herself.

It was a surprise to find so clean and comfortable a little dwelling in this New England wilderness. The young man had known the horrors of its most primitive housekeeping, and the dreary squalor of that level of society which does not rebel at the companionship of hens. This was the best thrift of an old-fashioned farmstead, though on such a small scale that it seemed like a hermitage. He listened eagerly to the old woman's quaint talk, he watched Sylvia's pale face and shining gray eyes with ever growing enthusiasm, and insisted that this was the best supper he had eaten for a month, and afterward, the new-made friends sat down in the doorway together while the moon came up.

Soon it would be berry-time, and Sylvia was a great help at picking. The cow was a good milker, though a plaguy thing to keep track of, the hostess gossiped frankly, adding presently that she had buried four children, so Sylvia's mother, and a son (who might be dead) in California were all the children she had left. "Dan, my boy, was a great hand to go gunning," she explained sadly. "I never wanted for pa'tridges or gray squer'ls while he was to home. He 's been a great wand'rer, I expect, and he 's no hand to write letters. There, I don't blame him, I 'd ha' seen the world myself if it had been so I could."

"Sylvia takes after him," the grandmother continued affectionately, after a minute's pause. "There ain't a foot o' ground she don't know her way over, and the wild creatur's counts her one o' themselves. Squer'ls she 'll tame to come an' feed right out o' her hands, and all sorts o' birds. Last winter she got the jay-birds to bangeing here, and I believe she 'd 'a' scanted herself of her own meals to have plenty to throw out amongst 'em, if I had n't kep' watch. Anything but crows, I tell her, I 'm willin' to help support—though Dan he had a tamed one o' them that did seem to have reason same as folks. It was round here a good spell after he went away. Dan an' his father they did n't hitch,—but he never held up his head ag'in after Dan had dared him an' gone off."

The guest did not notice this hint of family sorrows in his eager interest in something else.

"So Sylvy knows all about birds, does she?" he exclaimed, as he looked round at the little girl who sat, very demure but increasingly sleepy, in the moonlight. "I am making a collection of birds myself. I have been at it ever since I was a boy." (Mrs. Tilley smiled.) "There are two or three very rare ones I have been hunting for these five years. I mean to get them on my own ground if they can be found."

"Do you cage 'em up?" asked Mrs. Tilley doubtfully, in response to this enthusiastic announcement.

"Oh no, they 're stuffed and preserved, dozens and dozens of them," said the ornithologist, "and I have shot or snared every one myself. I caught a glimpse of a white heron a few miles from here on Saturday, and I have followed it in this direction. They have never been found in this district at all. The little white heron, it is," and he turned again to look at Sylvia with the hope of discovering that the rare bird was one of her acquaintances.

But Sylvia was watching a hop-toad in the narrow footpath.

"You would know the heron if you saw it," the stranger continued eagerly. "A queer tall white bird with soft feathers and long thin legs. And it would have a nest perhaps in the top of a high tree, made of sticks, something like a hawk's nest."

Sylvia's heart gave a wild beat; she knew that strange white bird, and had once stolen softly near where it stood in some bright green swamp grass, away over at the other side of the woods. There was an open place where the sunshine always seemed strangely yellow and hot, where tall, nodding rushes grew, and her grandmother had warned her that she might sink in the soft black mud underneath and never be heard of more. Not far beyond were the salt marshes and just this side the sea itself, which Sylvia wondered and dreamed much about, but never had seen, whose great voice could sometimes be heard above the noise of the woods on stormy nights.

"I can't think of anything I should like so much as to find that heron's nest," the handsome stranger was saying. "I would give ten dollars to anybody who could show it to me," he added desperately, "and I mean to spend my whole vacation hunting for it if need be. Perhaps it was only migrating, or had been chased out of its own region by some bird of prey."

Mrs. Tilley gave amazed attention to all this, but Sylvia still watched the toad, not divining, as she might have done at some calmer time, that the creature wished to get to its hole under the door-step, and was much hindered by the unusual spectators at that hour of the evening. No amount of thought, that night, could decide how many wished-for treasures the ten dollars, so lightly spoken of, would buy.

The next day the young sportsman hovered about the woods, and Sylvia kept him company, having lost her first fear of the friendly lad, who proved to be most kind and sympathetic. He told her many things about the birds and what they knew and where they lived and what they did with themselves. And he gave her a jack-knife, which she thought as great a treasure as if she were a desert-islander. All day long he did not once make her troubled or afraid except when he brought down some unsuspecting singing creature from its bough. Sylvia would have liked him vastly better without his gun; she could not understand why he killed the very birds he seemed to like so much. But as the day waned, Sylvia still watched the young man with loving admiration. She had never seen anybody so charming and delightful; the woman's heart, asleep in the child, was vaguely thrilled by a dream of love. Some premonition of that great power stirred and swayed these young creatures who traversed the solemn woodlands with soft-footed silent care. They stopped to listen to a bird's song; they pressed forward again eagerly, parting the branches—speaking to each other rarely and in whispers; the young man going first and Sylvia following, fascinated, a few steps behind, with her gray eyes dark with excitement.

She grieved because the longed-for white heron was elusive, but she did not lead the guest, she only followed, and there was no such thing as speaking first. The sound of her own unquestioned voice would have terrified her—it was hard enough to answer yes or no when there was need of that. At last evening began to fall, and they drove the cow home together, and Sylvia smiled with pleasure when they came to the place where she heard the whistle and was afraid only the night before.

II.

Half a mile from home, at the farther edge of the woods, where the land was highest, a great pine-tree stood, the last of its generation. Whether it was left for a boundary mark, or for what reason, no one could say; the woodchoppers who had felled its mates were dead and gone long ago, and a whole forest of sturdy trees, pines and oaks and maples, had grown again. But the stately head of this old pine towered above them all and made a landmark for sea and shore miles and miles away. Sylvia knew it well. She had always believed that whoever climbed to the top of it could see the ocean; and the little girl had often laid her hand on the great rough trunk and looked up wistfully at those dark boughs that the wind always stirred, no matter how hot and still the air might be below. Now she thought of the tree with a new excitement, for why, if one climbed it at break of day could not one see all the world, and easily discover from whence the white heron flew, and mark the place, and find the hidden nest?

What a spirit of adventure, what wild ambition! What fancied triumph and delight and glory for the later morning when she could make known the secret! It was almost too real and too great for the childish heart to bear.

All night the door of the little house stood open and the whip-poorwills came and sang upon the very step. The young sportsman and his old hostess were sound asleep, but Sylvia's great design kept her broad awake and watching. She forgot to think of sleep. The short summer night seemed as long as the winter darkness, and at last when the whippoorwills ceased, and she was afraid the morning would after all come too soon, she stole out of the house and followed the pasture path through the woods, hastening toward the open ground beyond, listening with a sense of comfort and companionship to the drowsy twitter of a half-awakened bird, whose perch she had jarred in passing. Alas, if the great wave of human interest which flooded for the first time this dull little life should sweep away the satisfactions of an existence heart to heart with nature and the dumb life of the forest!

There was the huge tree asleep yet in the paling moonlight, and small and silly Sylvia began with utmost bravery to mount to the top of it, with tingling, eager blood coursing the channels of her whole frame, with her bare feet and fingers, that pinched and held like bird's claws to the monstrous ladder reaching up, up, almost to the sky itself. First she must mount the white oak tree that grew alongside, where she was almost lost among the dark branches and the green leaves heavy and wet with dew; a bird fluttered off its nest, and a red squirrel ran to and fro and scolded pettishly at the harmless housebreaker. Sylvia felt her way easily. She had often climbed there, and knew that higher still one of the oak's upper branches chafed against the pine trunk, just where its lower boughs were set close together. There, when she made the dangerous pass from one tree to the other, the great enterprise would really begin.

She crept out along the swaying oak limb at last, and took the daring step across into the old pine-tree. The way was harder than she thought; she must reach far and hold fast, the sharp dry twigs caught and held her and scratched her like angry talons, the pitch made her thin little fingers clumsy and stiff as she went round and round the tree's great stem, higher and higher upward. The sparrows and robins in the woods below were beginning to wake and twitter to the dawn, yet it seemed much lighter there aloft in the pine-tree, and the child knew she must hurry if her project were to be of any use.

The tree seemed to lengthen itself out as she went up, and to reach farther and farther upward. It was like a great main-mast to the voyaging earth; it must truly have been amazed that morning through all its ponderous frame as it felt this determined spark of human spirit wending its way from higher branch to branch. Who knows how steadily the least twigs held themselves to advantage this light, weak creature on her way! The old pine must have loved his new dependent. More than all the hawks, and bats, and moths, and even the sweet voiced thrushes, was the brave, beating heart of the solitary gray-eyed child. And the tree stood still and frowned away the winds that June morning while the dawn grew bright in the east.

Sylvia's face was like a pale star, if one had seen it from the ground, when the last thorny bough was past, and she stood trembling and tired but wholly triumphant, high in the tree-top. Yes, there was the sea with the dawning sun making a golden dazzle over it, and toward that glorious east flew two hawks with slow-moving pinions. How low they looked in the air from that height when one had only seen them before far up, and dark against the blue sky. Their gray feathers were as soft as moths; they seemed only a little way from the tree, and Sylvia felt as if she too could go flying away among the clouds. Westward, the woodlands and farms reached miles and miles into the distance; here and there were church steeples, and white villages; truly it was a vast and awesome world!

The birds sang louder and louder. At last the sun came up bewilderingly bright. Sylvia could see the white sails of ships out at sea, and the clouds that were purple and rose-colored and yellow at first began to fade away. Where was the white heron's nest in the sea of green branches, and was this wonderful sight and pageant of the world the only reward for having climbed to such a giddy height? Now look down again, Sylvia, where the green marsh is set among the shining birches and dark hemlocks; there where you saw the white heron once you will see him again; look, look! a white spot of him like a single floating feather comes up from the dead hemlock and grows larger, and rises, and comes close at last, and goes by the landmark pine with steady sweep of wing and outstretched slender neck and crested head. And wait! wait! do not move a foot or a finger, little girl, do not send an arrow of light and consciousness from your two eager eyes, for the heron has perched on a pine bough not far beyond yours, and cries back to his mate on the nest and plumes his feathers for the new day!

The child gives a long sigh a minute later when a company of shouting cat-birds comes also to the tree, and vexed by their fluttering and lawlessness the solemn heron goes away. She knows his secret now, the wild, light, slender bird that floats and wavers, and goes back like an arrow presently to his home in the green world beneath. Then Sylvia, well satisfied, makes her perilous way down again, not daring to look far below the branch she stands on, ready to cry sometimes because her fingers ache and her lamed feet slip. Wondering over and over again what the stranger would say to her, and what he would think when she told him how to find his way straight to the heron's nest.

"Sylvy, Sylvy!" called the busy old grandmother again and again, but nobody answered, and the small husk bed was empty and Sylvia had disappeared.

The guest waked from a dream, and remembering his day's pleasure hurried to dress himself that might it sooner begin. He was sure from the way the shy little girl looked once or twice yesterday that she had at least seen the white heron, and now she must really be made to tell. Here she comes now, paler than ever, and her worn old frock is torn and tattered, and smeared with pine pitch. The grandmother and the sportsman stand in the door together and question her, and the splendid moment has come to speak of the dead hemlock-tree by the green marsh.

But Sylvia does not speak after all, though the old grandmother fretfully rebukes her, and the young man's kind, appealing eyes are looking straight in her own. He can make them rich with money; he has promised it, and they are poor now. He is so well worth making happy, and he waits to hear the story she can tell.

No, she must keep silence! What is it that suddenly forbids her and makes her dumb? Has she been nine years growing and now, when the great world for the first time puts out a hand to her, must she thrust it aside for a bird's sake? The murmur of the pine's green branches is in her ears, she remembers how the white heron came flying through the golden air and how they watched the sea and the morning together, and Sylvia cannot speak; she cannot tell the heron's secret and give its life away.

Dear loyalty, that suffered a sharp pang as the guest went away disappointed later in the day, that could have served and followed him and loved him as a dog loves! Many a night Sylvia heard the echo of his whistle haunting the pasture path as she came home with the loitering cow. She forgot even her sorrow at the sharp report of his gun and the sight of thrushes and sparrows dropping silent to the ground, their songs hushed and their pretty feathers stained and wet with blood. Were the birds better friends than their hunter might have been,—who can tell? Whatever treasures were lost to her, woodlands and summer-time, remember! Bring your gifts and graces and tell your secrets to this lonely country child!

Herman Melville

THE MAN-OF-WAR HAWK (1888)

Yon black man-of-war hawk that wheels in the light
O'er the black ship's white sky-s'l, sunned cloud to the sight,
Have we low-flyers wings to ascend to his height?

No arrow can reach him; nor thought can attain
To the placid supreme in the sweep of his reign.

THE BLUE-BIRD (LATE 1880S)

Beneath yon Larkspur's azure bells
That sun their bees in balmy air,
In mould no more the Blue-Bird dwells
Though late he found interment there.

All stiff he lay beneath the Fir
When shrill the March piped overhead.
And Pity gave him sepulchre
Within the Garden's sheltered bed.

And soft she sighed—Too soon he came;
On wings of hope he met the knell;
His heavenly tint the dust shall tame:
Ah, some misgiving had been well!

But, look, the clear etherial hue
In June it makes the Larkspur's dower;
It is the self-same welkin-blue—
The Bird's transfigured in the Flower!

Florence A. Merriam

WINTER WREN (1889)

ONE OCTOBER DAY when the raspberry patch was astir with fluttering kinglets and warblers, and noisy with the quarrying of white-throats, and the muttered excuses and *wait, wait* of tardy crows flying hurriedly over to the caucus in the next woods, I found the piquant little winter wrens bobbing about among the bushes oblivious to everything but their own particular business.

I gave one of them a start as I came on him unexpectedly, and so, on catching sight of a second, kept cautiously quiet. But, if you please, as soon as he got a glimpse of me, the inquisitive brown sprite came hurrying from one raspberry stem to another, with his absurd bit of a square tail over his back, and never once stopped till he got near enough for a good look. There he clung, atilt of a stem, bobbing his plump little body from side to side, half apologetically, but saying *quip* with an air that assured me he was afraid of no giants, however big! When I had admired his mottled, dusky vest and his rusty brown coat with its fine dusky barring, and noted the light line over his eye, and the white edging of his wing; and when he had decided to his satisfaction what I was doing there in the woods, he went hopping along, under an arching fern, off to the nearest stump.

When they are out hunting, their tails standing over their backs, their necks bent forward and their straight bills sticking out ahead, these little wrens have a most determined air! First you see one examining the sides and top of an old stump, running about, dipping down into the hollow, and then flitting off among the bushes, chattering *quip-quap* as he goes. Then one flies against the side of a tree to peck at a promising bit of bark and clambers several feet up the trunk to show what a good gymnast he is; and finally one pops up with a worm in his mouth, shakes it well before eating, and afterwards wipes his bill with the energy characteristic of the active, healthy temper of the whole wren family.

On the twelfth of October the ground was covered with snow, and the woods were so white and still I hardly expected to find anything in the raspberry patch. But walking through I discovered one of the little wrens, as active and busy as ever. As I stood watching him he climbed into the cosiest cover of leaves that a bush ever offered a bird for shelter, and I supposed he would settle himself to wait for the sun. But no! he examined it carefully, turning his head on one side and then the other, probably thinking it would be a very nice place for some tender worm, and then flew out into the cold snowy bushes again.

On the twenty-second of the month, when we had had a still heavier fall of snow, and the wrens found it too cold even to take dinner from a golden-rod stem, one of the confiding little birds came to hunt on the piazza right in front of my study window. You should have seen him work! He ignored the crumbs I threw out for him, but flitted about, running over the shrivelled vines trained over the piazza, and examining all the cracks and crannies where a fly might edge itself into the moulding. Once he dropped a worm, and you should have seen him come tumbling down after it!

The nest of this brave little bird is snug and warm, made of moss, lined with soft feathers, and lodged "in crevices of dead logs or stumps in thick, coniferous woods." What a pleasure it would be to follow him north, and study all his pretty ways in the dark forest home, where he furnishes mirth and sunshine all the summer through.

The wren is found in pigeon-hole No. 10, along with his cousins the thrasher and catbird. "Wrens, thrashers, etc.," is on the door-plate—perhaps the catbird is left out because he always takes pains to announce himself. All the household have long bills, and the catbird and thrasher have also long tails, with very short wings, while they all have a piquant way of perking up their tails when startled.

In contrast to the vireos, tanagers, and orioles, these birds spend most of their time in shrubs or bushes rather than in high trees. Different birds take various levels—stories in their out-of-doors house. The sparrows and chewinks live in the basement—on the ground-floor; the wrens and thrashers on the first floor in bushes and shrubs; the indigo-bird on the third floor—low trees; the vireos and tanagers and orioles on the fourth floor—high trees; while the swallows and swifts go above all—in the air.

Sidney Lanier

THE MOCKING BIRD (1891)

Superb and sole, upon a plumèd spray
   That o'er the general leafage boldly grew,
   He summ'd the woods in song; or typic drew
The watch of hungry hawks, the lone dismay
Of languid doves when long their lovers stray,
   And all birds' passion-plays that sprinkle dew
   At morn in brake or bosky avenue.
Whate'er birds did or dreamed, this bird could say.
Then down he shot, bounced airily along
The sward, twitched-in a grasshopper, made song
   Midflight, perched, primped, and to his art again.
   Sweet Science, this large riddle read me plain:
      How may the death of that dull insect be
      The life of yon trim Shakspere on the tree?

Frank M. Chapman

A WORD TO THE BEGINNER (1895)

How to Find Birds.—The best times of the day in which to look for birds are early morning and late afternoon. After a night of fasting and resting, birds are active and hungry. When their appetites are satisfied, they may rest quietly until hunger again sends them forth in search of food.

Experience will soon show you where birds are most abundant. The more varied the nature of the country the greater number of species you may expect to find inhabiting it. An ideal locality would be a bit of tree-dotted meadow with a reed-bordered pond or stream, surrounded by woods, rolling uplands and orchards.

Common sense will tell you how to act in the field. Birds are generally shy creatures and must be approached with caution. You must not, therefore, go observing or collecting dressed in flaming red, but in some inconspicuous garb and as quietly as a cat. Furthermore, go alone and keep the sun at your back—two apparently unrelated but equally important bits of advice.

The naturalist generally has the instincts of the hunter, and practice will develop them. The "squeak" is one of his most valuable aids. It is made by placing the lips to the back of the hand or finger and kissing vigorously. The sound produced bears some resemblance to the cries of a wounded or young bird. In the nesting season its utterance frequently creates much excitement in the bird-world, and at all times it is useful as a means of drawing bush- or reed-haunting species from their retreats. One may enter an apparently deserted thicket, and, after a few minutes' squeaking, find himself surrounded by an anxious or curious group of its feathered inhabitants.

The observer of birds will find that by far the best way to study their habits is to take a sheltered seat in some favored locality and become a part of the background. Your passage through the woods is generally attended by sufficient noise to warn birds of your coming long before you see them. They are then suspicious and ill at ease, but secrete yourself near some spot loved by birds, and it may be your privilege to learn the secrets of the forest. In this connection I cannot too highly recommend the observation blind described beyond. Adequate natural cover cannot always be found and at best, rarely permits of much freedom of movement. In it, one therefore becomes so cramped and tired that what should be a pleasure becomes hard labor. Whereas, I have passed as much as eight consecutive hours in a blind without undue fatigue; and, it may be added that, although I was in an open field only twenty feet from a Meadowlark's nest, the birds had not the slightest suspicion of my proximity.

How to Identify Birds.—Whether your object be to study birds as a scientist or simply as a lover of Nature, the first step is the same— you must learn to know them. This problem of identification has been given up in despair by many would-be ornithologists. We can neither pick, press, net, nor impale birds; and here the botanist and the entomologist have a distinct advantage. Even if we have the desire to resort to a gun, its use is not always possible. But with patience and practice the identification of birds is comparatively an easy matter, and in the end you will name them with surprising ease and certainty. There is generally more character in the flight of a bird than there is in the gait of a man. Both are frequently indescribable but perfectly diagnostic, and you learn to recognize bird friends as you do human ones—by experience.

———————

If you would "name the birds without a gun," by all means first visit a museum, and, with text-book in hand, study those species which you have previously found are to be looked for near your home. This preliminary introduction will serve to ripen your acquaintance in the field. A good field- or opera-glass is absolutely indispensable. Study your bird as closely as circumstances will permit, and write, *on the spot*, a comparative description of its size, the shape of its bill, tail, etc., and a detailed description of its colors. In describing form, take a Robin, Chipping Sparrow, or any bird you know, which best serves the purpose, as a basis for comparison. A bird's bill is generally its most diagnostic external character. A sketch of it in your note-book will frequently give you a good clue to its owner's family. It is of the utmost importance that descriptions and sketches should be made in the field. Not only do our memories sometimes deceive us, but we really see nothing with exactness until we attempt to describe it. Haunts, actions, and notes should also be carefully recorded.

Even better than a description is a figure colored with crayons or water-colors. It may be the crudest outline and in ridiculous pose, but at least it is definite. There is no possibility of error through the wrong use of terms; the observer draws or charts what he sees. Neither art nor skill is required. Anyone can learn to make the outline of the normal bird figure as readily as he can learn to make the letters of the alphabet, and a little practice will enable one to give the shape of bill, wings and tail, and even a hint of character-istic form and position. Typical, passerine outline figures may be made in advance in one's field note-book, and the shape of the bill and color may be added while the bird is under observation. A collection of diagrams or sketches of this kind will be found to possess far greater individuality and value than mere written descriptions. If the sketch cannot be completed, if essential details are lacking, it is obvious that the subject has not been seen with that definiteness upon which satisfactory field identification should rest.

GOLDFINCH (1895)

EXCEPT WHEN NESTING, Goldfinches are generally found in small flocks. Few birds seem to enjoy life more than these merry rovers. Every month brings them a change of fare, and in pursuit of fresh dainties the nesting-time is delayed almost until summer begins to wane.

Seed-bearing plants, whether in field or garden, form their larder; the old sunflowers rattle before their vigorous attack; the thistles spring into sudden blossom of black and gold as they swing from the nodding heads.

Their flight is expressive of their joyous nature, and as they bound through the air they hum a gay

Their love song is delivered with an ecstasy and abandon which carries them off their feet, and they circle over the fields sowing the air with music. The song has a canarylike character, and while it is less varied it possesses a wild, ringing quality wanting in the cage-bound bird's best efforts.

John Burroughs

WILD LIFE ABOUT MY CABIN (1904)

FRIENDS HAVE OFTEN asked me why I turned my back upon the Hudson and retreated into the wilderness. Well, I do not call it a retreat; I call it a withdrawal, a retirement, the taking up of a new position to renew the attack, it may be, more vigorously than ever. It is not always easy to give reasons. There are reasons within reasons, and often no reasons at all that we are aware of.

To a countryman like myself, not born to a great river or an extensive water-view, these things, I think, grow wearisome after a time. He becomes surfeited with a beauty that is alien to him. He longs for something more homely, private, and secluded. Scenery may be too fine or too grand and imposing for one's daily and hourly view. It tires after a while. It demands a mood that comes to you only at intervals. Hence it is never wise to build your house on the most ambitious spot in the landscape. Rather seek out a more humble and secluded nook or corner, which you can fill and warm with your domestic and home instincts and affections. In some things the half is often more satisfying than the whole. A glimpse of the Hudson River between hills or through openings in the trees wears better with me than a long expanse of it constantly spread out before me. One day I had an errand to a farmhouse nestled in a little valley or basin at the foot of a mountain. The earth put out protecting arms all about it,—a low hill with an orchard on one side, a sloping pasture on another, and the mountain, with the skirts of its mantling forests, close at hand in the rear. How my heart warmed toward it! I had been so long perched high upon the banks of a great river, in sight of all the world, exposed to every wind that blows, with a horizon-line that sweeps over half a county, that, quite unconsciously to myself, I was pining for a nook to sit down in. I was hungry for the private and the circumscribed; I knew it when I saw this sheltered farmstead. I had long been restless and dissatisfied,—a vague kind of homesickness; now I knew the remedy. Hence when, not long afterward, I was offered a tract of wild land, barely a mile from home, that contained a secluded nook and a few acres of level, fertile land shut off from the vain and noisy world of railroads, steamboats, and yachts by a wooded, precipitous mountain, I quickly closed the bargain, and built me a rustic house there, which I call "Slabsides," because its outer walls are covered with slabs. I might have given it a prettier name, but not one more fit, or more in keeping with the mood that brought me thither. A slab is the first cut from the log, and the bark goes with it. It is like the first cut from the loaf, which we call the crust, and which the children reject, but which we older ones often prefer. I wanted to take a fresh cut of life,—something that had the bark on, or, if you please, that was like a well-browned and hardened crust. After three years I am satisfied with the experiment. Life has a different flavor here. It is reduced to simpler terms; its complex equations all disappear. The exact value of x may still elude me, but I can press it hard; I have shorn it of many of its disguises and entanglements.

When I went into the woods the robins went with me, or rather they followed close. As soon as a space of ground was cleared and the garden planted, they were on hand to pick up the worms and insects, and to superintend the planting of the cherry-trees: three pairs the first summer, and more than double that number the second. In the third, their early morning chorus was almost as marked a feature as it is about the old farm homesteads. The robin is no hermit: he likes company; he likes the busy scenes of the farm and the village; he likes to carol to listening ears, and to build his nest as near your dwelling as he can. Only at rare intervals do I find a real sylvan robin, one that nests in the woods, usually by still waters, remote from human habitation. In such places his morning and evening carol is a welcome surprise to the fisherman or camper-out. It is like a dooryard flower found blooming in the wilderness. With the robins came the song sparrows and social sparrows, or chippies, also. The latter nested in the bushes near my cabin, and the song sparrows in the bank above the ditch that drains my land. I notice that Chippy finds just as many horsehairs to weave into her nest here in my horseless domain as she does when she builds in the open country. Her partiality for the long hairs from the manes and tails of horses and cattle is so great that she is often known as the hair-bird. What would she do in a country where there were neither cows nor horses? Yet these hairs are not good nesting-material. They are slippery, refractory things, and occasionally cause a tragedy in the nest by getting looped around the legs or the neck of the young or of the parent bird. They probably give a smooth finish to the interior, dear to the heart of Chippy.

The first year of my cabin life a pair of robins attempted to build a nest upon the round timber that forms the plate under my porch roof. But it was a poor place to build in. It took nearly a week's time and caused the birds a great waste of labor to find this out. The coarse material they brought for the foundation would not bed well upon the rounded surface of the timber, and every vagrant breeze that came along swept it off. My porch was kept littered with twigs and weed-stalks for days, till finally the birds abandoned the under-taking. The next season a wiser or more experienced pair made the attempt again, and succeeded. They placed the nest against the rafter where it joins the plate; they used mud from the start to level up with and to hold the first twigs and straws, and had soon completed a firm, shapely structure. When the young were about ready to fly, it was interesting to note that there was apparently an older and a younger, as in most families. One bird was more advanced than any of the others. Had the parent birds intentionally stimulated it with extra quantities of food, so as to be able to launch their offspring into the world one at a time? At any rate, one of the birds was ready to leave the nest a day and a half before any of the others. I happened to be looking at it when the first impulse to get outside the nest seemed to seize it. Its parents were encouraging it with calls and assurances from some rocks a few yards away. It answered their calls in vigorous, strident tones. Then it climbed over the edge of the nest upon the plate, took a few steps forward, then a few more, till it was a yard from the nest and near the end of the timber, and could look off into free space. Its parents apparently shouted, "Come on!" But its courage was not quite equal to the leap; it looked around, and seeing how far it was from home, scampered back to the nest, and climbed into it like a frightened child. It had made its first journey into the world, but the home tie had brought it quickly back. A few hours afterward it journeyed to the end of the plate again, and then turned and rushed back. The third time its heart was braver, its wings stronger, and leaping into the air with a shout, it flew easily to some rocks a dozen or more yards away. Each of the young in succession, at intervals of nearly a day, left the nest in this manner. There would be the first journey of a few feet along the plate, the first sudden panic at being so far from home, the rush back, a second and perhaps a third attempt, and then the irrevocable leap into the air, and a clamorous flight to a near-by bush or rock. Young birds never go back when they have once taken flight. The first free flap of the wing severs forever the ties that bind them to home.

The chickadees we have always with us. They are like the evergreens among the trees and plants. Winter has no terrors for them. They are properly wood-birds, but the groves and orchards know them also. Did they come near my cabin for better protection, or did they chance to find a little cavity in a tree there that suited them? Branch-builders and ground-builders are easily accommodated, but the chickadee must find a cavity, and a small one at that. The woodpeckers make a cavity when a suitable trunk or branch is found, but the chickadee, with its small, sharp beak, rarely does so; it usually smooths and deepens one already formed. This a pair did a few yards from my cabin. The opening was into the heart of a little sassafras, about four feet from the ground. Day after day the birds took turns in deepening and enlarging the cavity: a soft, gentle hammering for a few moments in the heart of the little tree, and then the appearance of the worker at the opening, with the chips in his, or her, beak. They changed off every little while, one working while the other gathered food. Absolute equality of the sexes, both in plumage and in duties, seems to prevail among these birds, as among a few other species. During the preparations for housekeeping the birds were hourly seen and heard, but as soon as the first egg was laid, all this was changed. They suddenly became very shy and quiet. Had it not been for the new egg that was added each day, one would have concluded that they had abandoned the place. There was a precious secret now that must be well kept. After incubation began, it was only by watching that I could get a glimpse of one of the birds as it came quickly to feed or to relieve the other.

One day a lot of Vassar girls came to visit me, and I led them out to the little sassafras to see the chickadees' nest. The sitting bird kept her place as head after head, with its nodding plumes and millinery, appeared above the opening to her chamber, and a pair of inquisitive eyes peered down upon her. But I saw that she was getting ready to play her little trick to frighten them away. Presently I heard a faint explosion at the bottom of the cavity, when the peeping girl jerked her head quickly back, with the exclamation, "Why, it spit at me!" The trick of the bird on such occasions is apparently to draw in its breath till its form perceptibly swells, and then give forth a quick, explosive sound like an escaping jet of steam. One involuntarily closes his eyes and jerks back his head. The girls, to their great amusement, provoked the bird into this pretty outburst of her impatience two or three times. But as the ruse failed of its effect, the bird did not keep it up, but let the laughing faces gaze till they were satisfied.

There is only one other bird known to me that resorts to the same trick to scare away intruders, and that is the great crested flycatcher. As your head appears before the entrance to the cavity in which the mother bird is sitting, a sudden burst of escaping steam seems directed at your face, and your backward movement leaves the way open for the bird to escape, which she quickly does.

The chickadee is a prolific bird, laying from six to eight eggs, and it seems to have few natural enemies. I think it is seldom molested by squirrels or black snakes or weasels or crows or owls. The entrance to the nest is usually so small that none of these creatures can come at them. Yet the number of chickadees in any given territory seems small. What keeps them in check? Probably the rigors of winter and a limited food-supply. The ant-eaters, fruit-eaters, and seed-eaters mostly migrate. Our all-the-year-round birds, like the chickadees, woodpeckers, jays, and nuthatches, live mostly on nuts and the eggs and larvæ of tree-insects, and hence their larder is a restricted one; hence, also, these birds rear only one brood in a season. A hairy woodpecker passed the winter in the woods near me by subsisting on a certain small white grub which he found in the bark of some dead hemlock-trees. He "worked" these trees,—four of them,—as the slang is, "for all they were worth." The grub was under the outer shell of bark, and the bird literally skinned the trees in getting at his favorite morsel. He worked from the top downward, hammering or prying off this shell, and leaving the trunk of the tree with a red, denuded look. Bushels of the fragments of the bark covered the ground at the foot of the tree in spring, and the trunk looked as if it had been flayed,—as it had.

The big chimney of my cabin of course attracted the chimney swifts, and as it was not used in summer, two pairs built their nests in it, and we had the muffled thunder of their wings at all hours of the day and night. One night, when one of the broods was nearly fledged, the nest that held them fell down into the fireplace. Such a din of screeching and chattering as they instantly set up! Neither my dog nor I could sleep. They yelled in chorus, stopping at the end of every half-minute as if upon signal. Now they were all screeching at the top of their voices, then a sudden, dead silence ensued. Then the din began again, to terminate at the instant as before. If they had been long practicing together, they could not have succeeded better. I never before heard the cry of birds so accurately timed. After a while I got up and put them back up the chimney, and stopped up the throat of the flue with newspapers. The next day one of the parent birds, in bringing food to them, came down the chimney with such force that it passed through the papers and brought up in the fireplace. On capturing it I saw that its throat was distended with food as a chipmunk's cheek with corn, or a boy's pocket with chestnuts. I opened its mandibles, when it ejected a wad of insects as large as a bean. Most of them were much macerated, but there were two houseflies yet alive and but little the worse for their close confinement. They stretched themselves, and walked about upon my hand, enjoying a breath of fresh air once more. It was nearly two hours before the swift again ventured into the chimney with food.

These birds do not perch, nor alight upon buildings or the ground. They are apparently upon the wing all day. They outride the storms. I have in my mind a cheering picture of three of them

I saw facing a heavy thunder-shower one afternoon. The wind was blowing a gale, the clouds were rolling in black, portentous billows out of the west, the peals of thunder were shaking the heavens, and the big drops were just beginning to come down, when, on looking up, I saw three swifts high in air, working their way slowly, straight into the teeth of the storm. They were not hurried or disturbed; they held themselves firmly and steadily; indeed, they were fairly at anchor in the air till the rage of the elements should have subsided. I do not know that any other of our land birds outride the storms in this way.

The phœbe-birds also soon found me out in my retreat, and a pair of them deliberated a long while about building on a little shelf in one of my gables. But, much to my regret, they finally decided in favor of a niche in the face of a ledge of rocks not far from my spring. The place was well screened by bushes and well guarded against the approach of snakes or four-footed prowlers, and the birds prospered well and reared two broods. They have now occupied the same nest three years in succession. This is unusual: Phœbe prefers a new nest each season, but in this case there is no room for another, and, the site being a choice one, she slightly repairs and refurnishes her nest each spring, leaving the new houses for her more ambitious neighbors.

Of wood-warblers my territory affords many specimens. One spring a solitary Nashville warbler lingered near my cabin for a week. I heard his bright, ringing song at all hours of the day. The next spring there were two or more, and they nested in my pea-bushes. The black and white creeping warblers are perhaps the most abundant. A pair of them built a nest in a steep moss and lichen covered hillside, beside a high gray rock. Our path to Julian's Rock led just above it. It was an ideal spot and an ideal nest, but it came to grief. Some small creature sucked the eggs. On removing the nest I found an earth-stained egg beneath it. Evidently the egg had ripened before its receptacle was ready, and the mother, for good luck, had placed it in the foundation.

One day, as I sat at my table writing, I had a call from the worm-eating warbler. It came into the open door, flitted about inquisitively, and then, startled by the apparition at the table, dashed against the window-pane and fell down stunned. I picked it up, and it lay with closed eyes panting in my hand. I carried it into the open air. In a moment or two it opened its eyes, looked about, and then closed them and fell to panting again. Soon it looked up at me once more and about the room, and seemed to say: "Where am I? What has happened to me?" Presently the panting ceased, the bird's breathing became more normal, it gradually got its bearings, and, at a motion of my hand, darted away. This is an abundant warbler in my vicinity, and nested this year near by. I have discovered that it has an air-song—the song of ecstasy—like that of the oven-bird. I had long suspected it, as I frequently heard a fine burst of melody that was new to me. One June day I was fortunate enough to see the bird delivering its song in the air above the low trees. As with the oven-bird, its favorite hour is the early twilight, though I hear the song occasionally at other hours. The bird darts upward fifty feet or more, about half the height that the oven-bird attains, and gives forth a series of rapid, ringing musical notes, which quickly glide into the long, sparrow-like trill that forms its ordinary workaday song. While this part is being uttered, the singer is on its downward flight into the woods. The flight-song of the oven-bird is louder and more striking, and is not so shy and furtive a performance. The latter I hear many times every June twilight, and I frequently see the singer reach his climax a hundred feet or more in the air, and then mark his arrow-like flight downward. I have heard this song also in the middle of the night near my cabin. At such times it stands out on the stillness like a bursting rocket on the background of the night.

One or two mornings in April, at a very early hour, I am quite sure to hear the hermit thrush singing in the bushes near my window. How quickly I am transported to the Delectable Mountains and to the mossy solitudes of the northern woods! The winter wren also pauses briefly in his northern journey, and surprises and delights my ear with his sudden lyrical burst of melody. Such a dapper, fidgety, gesticulating, bobbing-up-and-down-and-out-and-in little bird, and yet full of such sweet, wild melody! To get him at his best, one needs to hear him in a dim, northern hemlock wood, where his voice reverberates as in a great hall; just as one should hear the veery in a beech and birch wood, beside a purling trout brook, when the evening shades are falling. It then becomes to you the voice of some particular spirit of the place and the hour. The veery does not inhabit the woods immediately about my cabin, but in the summer twilight he frequently comes up from the valley below and sings along the borders of my territory. How welcome his simple flute-like strain! The wood thrush is the leading chorister in the woods about me. He does not voice the wildness, but seems to give a touch of something half rural, half urban,—such is the power of association in bird-songs. In the evening twilight I often sit on the highest point of the rocky rim of the great granite bowl that holds my three acres of prairie soil, and see the shadows deepen, and listen to the bird voices that rise up from the forest below me. The songs of many wood thrushes make a sort of golden warp in the texture of sounds that is being woven about me. Now the flight-song of the oven-bird holds the ear, then the fainter one of the worm-eating warbler lures it. The carol of the robin, the vesper hymn of the tanager, the flute of the veery, are all on the air. Finally, as the shadows deepen and the stars begin to come out, the whip-poor-will suddenly strikes up. What a rude intrusion upon the serenity and harmony of the hour! A cry without music, insistent, reiterated, loud, penetrating, and yet the ear welcomes it also; the night and the solitude are so vast that they can stand it; and when, an hour later, as the night enters into full possession, the bird comes and serenades me under my window or upon my doorstep, my heart warms toward it. Its cry is a love-call, and there is something of the ardor and persistence of love in it, and when the female responds, and comes and hovers near, there is an interchange of subdued, caressing tones between the two birds that it is a delight to hear. During my first summer here one bird used to strike up every night from a high ledge of rocks in front of my door. At just such a moment in the twilight he would begin, the first to break the stillness. Then the others would follow, till the solitude was vocal with their calls. They are rarely heard later than ten o'clock. Then at daybreak they take up the tale again, whipping poor Will till one pities him. One April morning between three and four o'clock, hearing one strike up near my window, I began counting its calls. My neighbor had told me he had heard one call over two hundred times without a break, which seemed to me a big story. But I have a much bigger one to tell. This bird actually laid upon the back of poor Will one thousand and eighty-eight blows, with only a barely perceptible pause here and there, as if to catch its breath. Then it stopped about half a minute and began again, uttering this time three hundred and ninety calls, when it paused, flew a little farther away, took up the tale once more, and continued till I fell asleep.

By day the whip-poor-will apparently sits motionless upon the ground. A few times in my walks through the woods I have started one up from almost under my feet. On such occasions the bird's movements suggest those of a bat; its wings make no noise, and it wavers about in an uncertain manner, and quickly drops to the ground again. One June day we flushed an old one with her two young, but there was no indecision or hesitation in the manner of the mother bird this time. The young were more than half fledged, and they scampered away a few yards and suddenly squatted upon the ground, where their protective coloring rendered them almost invisible. Then the anxious parent put forth all her arts to absorb our attention and lure us away from her offspring. She flitted before us from side to side, with spread wings and tail, now falling upon the ground, where she would remain a moment as if quite disabled, then perching upon an old stump or low branch with drooping, quivering wings, and imploring us by every gesture to take her and spare her young. My companion had his camera with him, but the bird would not remain long enough in one position for him to get her picture. The whip-poor-will builds no nest, but lays her two blunt, speckled eggs upon the dry leaves, where the plumage of the sitting bird blends perfectly with her surroundings. The eye, only a few feet away, has to search long and carefully to make her out. Every gray and brown and black tint of dry leaf and lichen, and bit of bark or broken twig, is copied in her plumage. In a day or two, after the young are hatched, the rnother begins to move about with them through the woods.

When I want the wild of a little different flavor and quality from that immediately about my cabin, I go a mile through the woods to Black Creek, here called the Shattega, and put my canoe into a long, smooth, silent stretch of water that winds through a heavily timbered marsh till it leads into Black Pond, an oval sheet of water half a mile or more across. Here I get the moist, spongy, tranquil, luxurious side of Nature. Here she stands or sits knee-deep in water, and wreathes herself with pond-lilies in summer, and bedecks herself with scarlet maples in autumn. She is an Indian maiden, dark, subtle, dreaming, with glances now and then that thrill the wild blood in one's veins. The Shattega here is a stream without banks and with a just perceptible current. It is a waterway through a timbered marsh. The level floor of the woods ends in an irregular line where the level surface of the water begins. As one glides along in his boat, he sees various rank aquatic growths slowly waving in the shadowy depths beneath him. The larger trees on each side unite their branches above his head, so that at times he seems to be entering an arboreal cave out of which glides the stream. In the more open places the woods mirror themselves in the glassy surface till one seems floating between two worlds, clouds and sky and trees below him matching those around and above him. A bird flits from shore to shore, and one sees it duplicated against the sky in the under-world. What vistas open! What banks of drooping foliage, what grain and arch of gnarled branches, lure the eye as one drifts or silently paddles along! The stream has absorbed the shadows so long that it is itself like a liquid shadow. Its bed is lined with various dark vegetable growths, as with the skin of some huge, shaggy animal, the fur of which slowly stirs in the languid current. I go here in early spring, after the ice has broken up, to get a glimpse of the first wild ducks and to play the sportsman without a gun. I am sure I would not exchange the quiet surprise and pleasure I feel, as, on rounding some point or curve in the stream, two or more ducks spring suddenly out from some little cove or indentation in the shore, and with an alarum *quack, quack*, launch into the air and quickly gain the free spaces above the treetops, for the satisfaction of the gunner who sees their dead bodies fall before his murderous fire. He has only a dead duck, which, the chances are, he will not find very toothsome at this season, while I have a live duck with whistling wings cleaving the air northward, where, in some lake or river of Maine or Canada, in late summer, I may meet him again with his brood. It is so easy, too, to bag the game with your eye, while your gun may leave you only a feather or two floating upon the water. The duck has wit, and its wit is as quick as, or quicker than, the sportsman's gun. One day in spring I saw a gunner cut down a duck when it had gained an altitude of thirty or forty feet above the stream. At the report it stopped suddenly, turned a somersault, and fell with a splash into the water. It fell like a brick, and disappeared like one; only a feather and a few bubbles marked the spot where it struck. Had it sunk? No; it had dived. It was probably winged, and in the moment it occupied in falling to the water it had decided what to do. It would go beneath the hunter, since it could not escape above him; it could fly in the water with only one wing, with its feet to aid it. The gunner instantly set up a diligent search in all directions, up and down along the shores, peering long and intently into the depths, thrusting his oar into the weeds and drift-wood at the edge of the water, but no duck or sign of duck could he find. It was as if the wounded bird had taken to the mimic heaven that looked so sunny and real down there, and gone on to Canada by that route. What astonished me was that the duck should have kept its presence of mind under such trying circumstances, and not have lost a fraction of a second of time in deciding on a course of action. The duck, I am convinced, has more sagacity than any other of our commoner fowl.

The day I see the first ducks I am pretty sure to come upon the first flock of blackbirds,—rusty grackles,—resting awhile on their northward journey amid the reeds, alders, and spice-bush beside the stream. They allow me to approach till I can see their yellow eyes and the brilliant iris on the necks and heads of the males. Many of them are vocal, and their united voices make a volume of sound that is analogous to a bundle of slivers. Sputtering, splintering, rasping, rending, their notes chafe and excite the ear. They suggest thorns and briers of sound, and yet are most welcome. What voice that rises from our woods or beside our waters in April is not tempered or attuned to the ear? Just as I like to chew the crinkleroot and the twigs of the spice-bush at this time, or at any time, for that matter, so I like to treat my ear to these more aspirated and astringent bird voices. Is it Thoreau who says they are like pepper and salt to this sense? In all the blackbirds we hear the voice of April not yet quite articulate; there is a suggestion of catarrh and influenza still in the air-passages. I should, perhaps, except the red-shouldered starling, whose clear and liquid *gur-ga-lee* or *o-ka-lee*, above the full water-courses, makes a different impression. The cowbird also has a clear note, but it seems to be wrenched or pumped up with much effort.

In May I go to Black Creek to hear the warblers and the water-thrushes. It is the only locality where I have ever heard the two water-thrushes, or accentors, singing at the same time,—the New York and the large-billed. The latter is much more abundant and much the finer songster. How he does make these watery solitudes ring with his sudden, brilliant burst of song! But the more northern species pleases the ear also with his quieter and less hurried strain. I drift in my boat and let the ear attend to the one, then to the other, while the eye takes note of their quick, nervous movements and darting flight. The smaller species probably does not nest along this stream, but the large-billed breeds here abundantly. The last nest I found was in the roots of an upturned tree, with the water immediately beneath it. I had asked a neighboring farm-boy if he knew of any birds' nests.

"Yes," he said; and he named over the nests of robins, highholes, sparrows, and others, and then that of a "tip-up."

At this last I pricked up my ears, so to speak. I had not seen a tip-up's nest in many a day. "Where?" I inquired.

"In the roots of a tree in the woods," said Charley.

"Not the nest of the 'tip-up,' or sandpiper," said I. "It builds on the ground in the open country near streams."

"Anyhow, it tipped," replied the boy.

He directed me to the spot, and I found, as I expected to find, the nest of the water-thrush. When the Vassar girls came again, I conducted them to the spot, and they took turns in walking a small tree trunk above the water, and gazing upon a nest brimming with the downy backs of young birds.

When I am listening to the water-thrushes, I am also noting with both eye and ear the warblers and vireos. There comes a week in May when the speckled Canada warblers are in the ascendant. They feed in the low bushes near the water's edge, and are very brisk and animated in voice and movement. The eye easily notes their slate-blue backs and yellow breasts with their broad band of black spots, and the ear quickly discriminates their not less marked and emphatic song.

In late summer I go to the Shattega, and to the lake out of which it flows, for white pond-lilies, and to feast my eye on the masses of purple loosestrife and the more brilliant but more hidden and retired cardinal-flower that bloom upon its banks. One cannot praise the pond-lily; his best words mar it, like the insects that eat its petals: but he can contemplate it as it opens in the morning sun and distills such perfume, such purity, such snow of petal and such gold of anther, from the dark water and still darker ooze. How feminine it seems beside its coarser and more robust congeners; how shy, how pliant, how fine in texture and star-like in form!

The loosestrife is a foreign plant, but it has made itself thoroughly at home here, and its masses of royal purple make the woods look civil and festive. The cardinal burns with a more intense fire, and fairly lights up the little dark nooks where it glasses itself in the still water. One must pause and look at it. Its intensity, its pure scarlet, the dark background upon which it is projected, its image in the still darker water, and its general air of retirement and seclusion, all arrest and delight the eye. It is a heart-throb of color on the bosom of the dark solitude.

The rarest and wildest animal that my neighborhood boasts of is the otter. Every winter we see the tracks of one or more of them upon the snow along Black Creek. But the eye that has seen the animal itself in recent years I cannot find. It probably makes its excursions along the creek by night. Follow its track—as large as that of a fair-sized dog—over the ice, and you will find that it ends at every open pool and rapid, and begins again upon the ice beyond. Sometimes it makes little excursions up the bank, its body often dragging in the snow like a log. My son followed the track one day far up the mountain-side, where the absence of the snow caused him to lose it. I like to think of so wild and shy a creature holding its own within sound of the locomotive's whistle.

The fox passes my door in winter, and probably in summer too, as do also the 'possum and the coon. The latter tears down my sweet corn in the garden, and the rabbit eats off my raspberry-bushes and nibbles my first strawberries, while the woodchucks eat my celery and beans and peas. Chipmunks carry off the corn I put out for the chickens, and weasels eat the chickens themselves.

Many times during the season I have in my solitude a visit from a bald eagle. There is a dead tree near the summit, where he often perches, and which we call the "old eagle-tree." It is a pine, killed years ago by a thunderbolt,—the bolt of Jove,—and now the bird of Jove hovers about it or sits upon it. I have little doubt that what attracted me to this spot attracts him,—the seclusion, the savageness, the elemental grandeur. Sometimes, as I look out of my window early in the morning, I see the eagle upon his perch, preening his plumage, or waiting for the rising sun to gild the mountain-tops. When the smoke begins to rise from my chimney, or he sees me going to the spring for water, he concludes it is time for him to be off. But he need not fear the crack of the rifle here; nothing more deadly than field-glasses shall be pointed at him while I am about. Often in the course of the day I see him circling above my domain, or winging his way toward the mountains. His home is apparently in the Shawangunk Range, twenty or more miles distant, and I fancy he stops or lingers above me on his way to the river. The days on which I see him are not quite the same as the other days. I think my thoughts soar a little higher all the rest of the morning: I have had a visit from a messenger of Jove. The lift or range of those great wings has passed into my thought. I once heard a collector get up in a scientific body and tell how many eggs of the bald eagle he had clutched that season, how many from this nest, how many from that, and how one of the eagles had deported itself after he had killed its mate. I felt ashamed for him. He had only proved himself a superior human weasel. The man with the rifle and the man with the collector's craze are fast reducing the number of eagles in the country. Twenty years ago I used to see a dozen or more along the river in the spring when the ice was breaking up, where I now see only one or two, or none at all. In the present case, what would it profit me could I find and plunder my eagle's nest, or strip his skin from his dead carcass? Should I know him better? I do not want to know him that way. I want rather to feel the inspiration of his presence and noble bearing. I want my interest and sympathy to go with him in his continental voyaging up and down, and in his long, elevated flights to and from his eyrie upon the remote, solitary cliffs. He draws great lines across the sky; he sees the forests like a carpet beneath him, he sees the hills and valleys as folds and wrinkles in a many-colored tapestry; he sees the river as a silver belt connecting remote horizons. We climb mountain-peaks to get a glimpse of the spectacle that is hourly spread out beneath him. Dignity, elevation, repose, are his. I would have my thoughts take as wide a sweep. I would be as far removed from the petty cares and turmoils of this noisy and blustering world.

Theodore Roosevelt

FROM *AN AUTOBIOGRAPHY* (1913)

S AGAMORE HILL takes its name from the old Sagamore Mohan-nis, who, as chief of his little tribe, signed away his rights to the land two centuries and a half ago. The house stands right on the top of the hill, separated by fields and belts of woodland from all other houses, and looks out over the bay and the Sound. We see the sun go down beyond long reaches of land and of water. Many birds dwell in the trees round the house or in the pastures and the woods near by, and of course in winter gulls, loons, and wild fowl frequent the waters of the bay and the Sound. We love all the seasons; the snows and bare woods of winter; the rush of growing things and the blossom-spray of spring; the yellow grain, the ripening fruits and tasseled corn, and the deep, leafy shades that are heralded by "the green dance of summer"; and the sharp fall winds that tear the brilliant banners with which the trees greet the dying year.

Most of the birds in our neighborhood are the ordinary home friends of the house and the barn, the wood lot and the pasture; but now and then the species make queer shifts. The cheery quail, alas! are rarely found near us now; and we no longer hear the whip-poor-wills at night. But some birds visit us now which formerly did not. When I was a boy neither the black-throated green warbler nor the purple finch nested around us, nor were bobolinks found in our fields. The black-throated green warbler is now one of our commonest summer warblers; there are plenty of purple finches; and, best of all, the bobolinks are far from infrequent. I had written about these new visitors to John Burroughs, and once when he came out to see me I was able to show them to him.

When I was President, we owned a little house in western Virginia; a delightful house, to us at least, although only a shell of rough boards. We used sometimes to go there in the fall, perhaps at Thanksgiving, and on these occasions we would have quail and rabbits of our own shooting, and once in a while a wild turkey. We also went there in the spring. Of course many of the birds were different from our Long Island friends. There were mocking-birds, the most attractive of all birds, and blue grosbeaks, and cardinals and summer redbirds, instead of scarlet tanagers, and those wonderful singers the Bewick's wrens, and Carolina wrens. All these I was able to show John Burroughs when he came to visit us; although, by the way, he did not appreciate as much as we did one set of inmates of the cottage—the flying squirrels. We loved having the flying squirrels, father and mother and half-grown young, in their nest among the rafters; and at night we slept so soundly that we did not in the least mind the wild gambols of the little fellows through the rooms, even when, as sometimes happened, they would swoop down to the bed and scuttle across it.

John Muir

A NEW WORLD (1913)

To this charming hut, in the sunny woods, overlooking a flowery glacier meadow and a lake rimmed with white water-lilies, we were hauled by an ox-team across trackless carex swamps and low rolling hills sparsely dotted with round-headed oaks. Just as we arrived at the shanty, before we had time to look at it or the scenery about it, David and I jumped down in a hurry off the load of household goods, for we had discovered a blue jay's nest, and in a minute or so we were up the tree beside it, feasting our eyes on the beautiful green eggs and beautiful birds,—our first memorable discovery. The handsome birds had not seen Scotch boys before and made a desperate screaming as if we were robbers like themselves; though we left the eggs untouched, feeling that we were already beginning to get rich, and wondering how many more nests we should find in the grand sunny woods. Then we ran along the brow of the hill that the shanty stood on, and down to the meadow, searching the trees and grass tufts and bushes, and soon discovered a bluebird's and a woodpecker's nest, and began an acquaintance with the frogs and snakes and turtles in the creeks and springs.

This sudden plash into pure wildness—baptism in Nature's warm heart—how utterly happy it made us! Nature streaming into us, wooingly teaching her wonderful glowing lessons, so unlike the dismal grammar ashes and cinders so long thrashed into us. Here without knowing it we still were at school; every wild lesson a love lesson, not whipped but charmed into us. Oh, that glorious Wisconsin wilderness! Everything new and pure in the very prime of the spring when Nature's pulses were beating highest and mysteriously keeping time with our own! Young hearts, young leaves, flowers, animals, the winds and the streams and the sparkling lake, all wildly, gladly rejoicing together!

Next morning, when we climbed to the precious jay nest to take another admiring look at the eggs, we found it empty. Not a shell-fragment was left, and we wondered how in the world the birds were able to carry off their thin-shelled eggs either in their bills or in their feet without breaking them, and how they could be kept warm while a new nest was being built. Well, I am still asking these questions. When I was on the Harriman Expedition I asked Robert Ridgway, the eminent ornithologist, how these sudden flittings were accomplished, and he frankly confessed that he didn't know, but guessed that jays and many other birds carried their eggs in their mouths; and when I objected that a jay's mouth seemed too small to hold its eggs, he replied that birds' mouths were larger than the narrowness of their bills indicated. Then I asked him what he thought they did with the eggs while a new nest was being prepared. He didn't know; neither do I to this day. A specimen of the many puzzling problems presented to the naturalist.

We soon found many more nests belonging to birds that were not half so suspicious. The handsome and notorious blue jay plunders the nests of other birds and of course he could not trust us. Almost all the others—brown thrushes, bluebirds, song sparrows, kingbirds, hen-hawks, nighthawks, whip-poor-wills, woodpeckers, etc.—simply tried to avoid being seen, to draw or drive us away, or paid no attention to us.

NORTH FORK OF THE MERCED (1911)

I HAVE BEEN MAKING the acquaintance of a very interesting little
bird that flits about the falls and rapids of the main branches of
the river. It is not a water-bird in structure, though it gets its living
in the water, and never leaves the streams. It is not web-footed, yet
it dives fearlessly into deep swirling rapids, evidently to feed at the
bottom, using its wings to swim with under water just as ducks and
loons do. Sometimes it wades about in shallow places, thrusting its
head under from time to time in a jerking, nodding, frisky way that
is sure to attract attention. It is about the size of a robin, has short
crisp wings serviceable for flying either in water or air, and a tail of
moderate size slanted upward, giving it, with its nodding, bobbing
manners, a wrennish look. Its color is plain bluish ash, with a tinge
of brown on the head and shoulders. It flies from fall to fall, rapid
to rapid, with a solid whir of wing-beats like those of a quail, follows
the windings of the stream, and usually alights on some rock jutting
up out of the current, or on some stranded snag, or rarely on the
dry limb of an overhanging tree, perching like regular tree birds
when it suits its convenience. It has the oddest, daintiest mincing
manners imaginable; and the little fellow can sing too, a sweet,
thrushy, fluty song, rather low, not the least boisterous, and much
less keen and accentuated than from its vigorous briskness one
would be led to look for. What a romantic life this little bird leads
on the most beautiful portions of the streams, in a genial climate
with shade and cool water and spray to temper the summer heat.
No wonder it is a fine singer, considering the stream songs it hears
day and night. Every breath the little poet draws is part of a song,
for all the air about the rapids and falls is beaten into music, and
its first lessons must begin before it is born by the thrilling and

quivering of the eggs in unison with the tones of the falls. I have not yet found its nest, but it must be near the streams, for it never leaves them.

Robert Frost

THE OVEN BIRD (1916)

There is a singer everyone has heard,
Loud, a mid-summer and a mid-wood bird,
Who makes the solid tree trunks sound again.
He says that leaves are old and that for flowers
Mid-summer is to spring as one to ten.
He says the early petal-fall is past
When pear and cherry bloom went down in showers
On sunny days a moment overcast;
And comes that other fall we name the fall.
He says the highway dust is over all.
The bird would cease and be as other birds
But that he knows in singing not to sing.
The question that he frames in all but words
Is what to make of a diminished thing.

Carl Sandburg

PURPLE MARTINS (1920)

If we were such and so, the same as these,
maybe we too would be slingers and sliders,
tumbling half over in the water mirrors,
tumbling half over at the horse heads of the sun,
tumbling our purple numbers.

Twirl on, you and your satin blue.
Be water birds, be air birds.
Be these purple tumblers you are.

     Dip and get away
From loops into slip-knots,
Write your own ciphers and figure eights.
It is your wooded island here in Lincoln park.
Everybody knows this belongs to you.

     Five fat geese
Eat grass on a sod bank
And never count your slinging ciphers,
              your sliding figure eights,

A man on a green paint iron bench,
Slouches his feet and sniffs in a book,
And looks at you and your loops and slip-knots,

And looks at you and your sheaths of satin blue,
And slouches again and sniffs in the book,
And mumbles: It is an idle and a doctrinaire exploit.
Go on tumbling half over in the water mirrors.
Go on tumbling half over at the horse heads of the sun.
>   Be water birds, be air birds.
>   Be these purple tumblers you are.

John Hall Wheelock

THE FISH-HAWK (1922)

On the large highway of the awful air that flows
   Unbounded between sea and heaven, while twilight screened
The sorrowful distances, he moved and had repose;
   On the huge wind of the Immensity he leaned
His steady body in long lapse of flight—and rose

Gradual, through broad gyres of ever-climbing rest,
   Up the clear stair of the eternal sky, and stood
Throned on the summit! Slowly, with his widening breast,
   Widened around him the enormous Solitude,
From the gray rim of ocean to the glowing west.

Headlands and capes forlorn of the far coast, the land
   Rolling her barrens toward the south, he, from his throne
Upon the gigantic wind, beheld: he hung—he fanned
   The abyss for mighty joy, to feel beneath him strown
Pale pastures of the sea, with heaven on either hand—

The world with all her winds and waters, earth and air,
   Fields, folds, and moving clouds. The awful and adored
Arches and endless aisles of vacancy, the fair
   Void of sheer heights and hollows hailed him as her lord
And lover in the highest, to whom all heaven lay bare!

Till from that tower of ecstasy, that baffled height,
    Stooping, he sank; and slowly on the world's wide way
Walked, with great wing on wing, the merciless, proud Might,
    Hunting the huddled and lone reaches for his prey
Down the dim shore—and faded in the crumbling light.

Slowly the dusk covered the land. Like a great hymn
    The sound of moving winds and waters was; the sea
Whispered a benediction, and the west grew dim
    Where evening lifted her clear candles quietly . . .
Heaven, crowded with stars, trembled from rim to rim.

Marianne Moore

THE FRIGATE PELICAN (1935)

Rapidly cruising or lying on the air there is a bird
   that realizes Rasselas's friend's project
  of wings uniting levity with strength. This
    hell-diver, frigate bird, hurricane-
bird; unless swift is the proper word
    for him, the storm omen when
  he flies close to the waves, should be seen
    fishing, although oftener
    he appears to prefer

to take, on the wing, from industrious crude-winged species,
   the fish they have caught, and is seldom successless.
   A marvel of grace, no matter how fast his
    victim may fly or how often may
turn. The others with similar ease,
   slowly rising once more,
    move out to the top
    of the circle and stop

and blow back, allowing the wind to reverse their direction—
   unlike the more stalwart swan that can ferry the
   woodcutter's two children home. Make hay; keep
    the shop; I have one sheep; were a less

limber animal's mottoes. This one
    finds sticks for the swan's-down dress
of his child to rest upon and would
      not know Gretel from Hänsel.
      As impassioned Handel—

meant for a lawyer and a masculine German domestic
   career—clandestinely studied the harpsichord
   and never was known to have fallen in love,
     the unconfiding frigate bird hides
in the height and in the majestic
     display of his art. He glides
   a hundred feet or quivers about
     as charred paper behaves—full
     of feints; and an eagle

of vigilance. . . . *Festina lente.* Be gay
   civilly? How so? "If I do well I am blessed
   whether any bless me or not, and if I do
     ill I am cursed." We watch the moon rise
on the Susquehanna. In his way,
     this most romantic bird flies
to a more mundane place, the mangrove
     swamp to sleep. He wastes the moon.
     But he, and others, soon

rise from the bough and though flying, are able to foil the tired
   moment of danger that lays on heart and lungs the
   weight of the python that crushes to powder.

Rachel Carson

FLOOD TIDE (1941)

WITH THE DUSK a strange bird came to the island from its nesting grounds on the outer banks. Its wings were pure black, and from tip to tip their spread was more than the length of a man's arm. It flew steadily and without haste across the sound, its progress as measured and as meaningful as that of the shadows which little by little were dulling the bright water path. The bird was called Rynchops, the black skimmer.

As he neared the shore of the island the skimmer drifted closer to the water, bringing his dark form into strong silhouette against the gray sheet, like the shadow of a great bird that passed unseen above. Yet so quietly did he approach that the sound of his wings, if sound there were, was lost in the whisper song of the water turning over the shells on the wet sand.

At the last spring tide, when the thin shell of the new moon brought the water lapping among the sea oats that fringed the dunes of the banks, Rynchops and his kin had arrived on the outer barrier strip of sand between sound and sea. They had journeyed northward from the coast of Yucatan where they had wintered. Under the warm June sun they would lay their eggs and hatch their buff-colored chicks on the sandy islands of the sound and on the outer beaches. But at first they were weary after the long flight and they rested by day on sand bars when the tide was out or roamed over the sound and its bordering marshes by night.

Before the moon had come to the full, Rynchops had remembered the island. It lay across a quiet sound from which the banks shouldered away the South Atlantic rollers. To the north the island was separated from the mainland by a deep gutter where the ebbing tides raced strongly. On the south side the beach sloped gently, so that at slack water the fishermen could wade out half a mile before the water came above their armpits as they raked scallops or hauled their long seines. In these shallows young fishes swarmed, feeding on the small game of the waters, and shrimp swam with backward flipping of their tails. The rich life of the shallows brought the skimmers nightly from their nesting grounds on the banks, to take their food from the water as they moved with winnowing flight above it.

About sunset the tide had been out. Now it was rising, covering the afternoon resting places of the skimmers, moving through the inlet, and flowing up into the marshes. Through most of the night the skimmers would feed, gliding on slender wings above the water in search of the small fishes that had moved in with the tide to the shelter of grassy shallows. Because they fed on the rising tide, the skimmers were called flood gulls.

On the south beach of the island, where water no deeper than a man's hand ran over gently ribbed bottom, Rynchops began to wheel and quarter over the shallows. He flew with a curious, lilting motion, lifting his wings high after the downstroke. His head was bent sharply so that the long lower bill, shaped like a scissor blade, might cut the water.

The blade or cutwater plowed a miniature furrow over the placid sheet of the sound, setting up wavelets of its own and sending vibrations thudding down through the water to rebound from the sandy bottom. The wave messages were received by the blennies and killifish that were roving the shallows on the alert for food. In the fish world many things are told by sound waves. Sometimes the vibrations tell of food animals like small shrimps or oar-footed crustaceans moving in swarms overhead. And so at the passing of the skimmer the small fishes came nosing at the surface, curious and hungry. Rynchops, wheeling about, returned along the way he had come and snapped up three of the fishes by the rapid opening and closing of his short upper bill.

Ah-h-h-h, called the black skimmer. *Ha-a-a-a! Ha-a-a-a! Ha-a-a-a!* His voice was harsh and barking. It carried far across the water, and from the marshes there came back, like echoes, the answering cries of other skimmers.

While the water was reclaiming inch after inch of sandy shore, Rynchops moved back and forth over the south beach of the island, luring the fishes to rise along his path and seizing them on his return. After he had taken enough minnows to appease his hunger he wheeled up from the water with half a dozen flapping wing beats and circled the island. As he soared above the marshy eastern end schools of killifish moved beneath him through the forests of sea hay, but they were safe from the skimmer, whose wingspread was too great to allow him to fly among the clumps of grass.

Rynchops swerved out around the dock that had been built by the fisherman who lived on the island, crossed the gutter, and swept far over the silt marshes, taking joy in flight and soaring motion. There he joined a flock of other skimmers and together they moved over the marshes in long lines and columns, sometimes appearing as dark shadows on the night sky; sometimes as spectral birds when, wheeling swallowlike in air, they showed white breasts and gleaming underparts. As they flew they raised their voices in the weird night chorus of the skimmers, a strange medley of notes high-pitched and low, now soft as the cooing of a mourning dove, and again harsh as the cawing of a crow; the whole chorus rising and falling, swelling and throbbing, dying away in the still air like the far-off baying of a pack of hounds.

The flood gulls circled the island and crossed and recrossed the flats to the southward. All through the hours of the rising tide, they would hunt in flocks over the quiet waters of the sound. The skimmers loved nights of darkness and tonight thick clouds lay between the water and the moon's light.

Theodore Roethke

THE HERON (1941)

The heron stands in water where the swamp
Has deepened to the blackness of a pool,
Or balances with one leg on a hump
Of marsh grass heaped above a musk-rat hole.

He walks the shallow with an antic grace.
The great feet break the ridges of the sand,
The long eye notes the minnow's hiding place.
His beak is quicker than a human hand.

He jerks a frog across his bony lip,
Then points his heavy bill above the wood.
The wide wings flap but once to lift him up.
A single ripple starts from where he stood.

Aldo Leopold

Illustrations by Charles W. Schwartz

APRIL: SKY DANCE (1949)

I OWNED MY FARM for two years before learning that the sky dance is to be seen over my woods every evening in April and May. Since we discovered it, my family and I have been reluctant to miss even a single performance.

The show begins on the first warm evening in April at exactly 6:50 P.M. The curtain goes up one minute later each day until 1 June, when the time is 7:50. This sliding scale is dictated by vanity, the dancer demanding a romantic light intensity of exactly 0.05 foot-candles. Do not be late, and sit quietly, lest he fly away in a huff.

The stage props, like the opening hour, reflect the temperamental demands of the performer. The stage must be an open amphitheater in woods or brush, and in its center there must be a mossy spot, a streak of sterile sand, a bare outcrop of rock, or a bare roadway. Why the male woodcock should be such a stickler for a bare dance floor puzzled me at first, but I now think it is a matter of legs. The woodcock's legs are short, and his struttings cannot be executed to advantage in dense grass or weeds, nor could his lady see them there. I have more woodcocks than most farmers because I have more mossy sand, too poor to support grass.

Knowing the place and the hour, you seat yourself under a bush to the east of the dance floor and wait, watching against the sunset for the woodcock's arrival. He flies in low from some neighboring

thicket, alights on the bare moss, and at once begins the overture;
a series of queer throaty *peents* spaced about two seconds apart, and
sounding much like the summer call of the nighthawk.

Suddenly the peenting ceases and the bird flutters skyward in a
series of wide spirals, emitting a musical twitter. Up and up he goes,

the spirals steeper and smaller, the twittering louder and louder, until the performer is only a speck in the sky. Then, without warning, he tumbles like a crippled plane, giving voice in a soft liquid warble that a March bluebird might envy. At a few feet from the ground he levels off and returns to his peenting ground, usually to the exact spot where the performance began, and there resumes his peenting.

It is soon too dark to see the bird on the ground, but you can see his flights against the sky for an hour, which is the usual duration of the show. On moonlit nights, however, it may continue, at intervals, as long as the moon continues to shine.

At daybreak the whole show is repeated. In early April the final curtain falls at 5:15 A.M.; the time advances two minutes a day until June, when the performance closes for the year at 3:15. Why the disparity in sliding scale? Alas, I fear that even romance tires, for it takes only a fifth as much light to stop the sky dance at dawn as suffices to start it at sunset.

* * *

It is fortunate, perhaps, that no matter how intently one studies the hundred little dramas of the woods and meadows, one can never learn all of the salient facts about any one of them. What I do not yet know about the sky dance is: where is the lady, and just what part, if any, does she play? I often see two woodcocks on a peenting ground, and the two sometimes fly together, but they never peent together. Is the second bird the hen, or a rival male?

Another unknown: is the twitter vocal, or is it mechanical? My friend Bill Feeney once clapped a net over a peenting bird and removed his outer primary wing feathers; thereafter the bird peented and warbled, but twittered no more. But one such experiment is hardly conclusive.

Another unknown: up to what stage of nesting does the male continue the sky dance? My daughter once saw a bird peenting within twenty yards of a nest containing hatched eggshells, but was this *his* lady's nest? Or is this secretive fellow possibly bigamous without our ever having found it out? These, and many other questions, remain mysteries of the deepening dusk.

The drama of the sky dance is enacted nightly on hundreds of farms, the owners of which sigh for entertainment, but harbor the illusion that it is to be sought in theaters. They live on the land, but not by the land.

The woodcock is a living refutation of the theory that the utility of a game bird is to serve as a target, or to pose gracefully on a slice of toast. No one would rather hunt woodcock in October than I, but since learning of the sky dance I find myself calling one or two birds enough. I must be sure that, come April, there be no dearth of dancers in the sunset sky.

Roger Tory Peterson & James Fisher

KITES OVER THE SAWGRASS (1956)

OKEECHOBEE MEANS in Seminole "Big Water." Any word in the Seminole Indian language ending in double *e* denotes water: *Kissimmee*, winding water; *Pahayokee*, grassy water; *wampee*, a water plant (pickerelweed); *hatchee*, river.

Lake Okeechobee, with an average depth of only five or six feet, sprawls over an area of 700 square miles. Although the highway completely encircles it, for great stretches the lake itself is hidden from the motorists' view by a 20-foot dyke built to prevent a repetition of the disasters of 1926 and 1928. Thirty-six hundred people lost their lives when hurricanes of incredible violence pushed the waters of the lake over the settlements on the southeast and west shores. In the little town of Moore Haven, 1500 people drowned. It is said that these two storms were among the principal causes of the collapse of the "Florida Boom" of the twenties.

There is a vast loneliness about the big water; its featureless horizons suggest the ocean or the Great Plains, domed over by 180 degrees of unobstructed sky. It lies between two blank spots on the map of Florida, two great areas almost devoid of towns and roads. To the south lie the Everglades, which it once nourished with its overflow; to the north the Kissimmee Prairie, through which we had driven on the endlessly straight road. Ecologically the Kissimmee Prairie is like a displaced part of the American west. Cowboys, booted and spurred, peered at us from under their broad-brimmed

Stetsons. And the sandhill cranes and burrowing owls almost gave the illusion that we were in Montana or Wyoming. However, the grass is much longer and coarser.

At Clewiston, on the south side of the lake where the Caloosa-hatchee breaches the dyke and carries off the overflow, we again went out onto the lake. Once within the great earth wall we were completely cut off from civilization. No cottages dotted the shore. Flat marshes, cane patches, and lotus beds extended great distances out into the lake until open water shimmered to the empty horizon. It was in the hope of seeing America's fourth-rarest bird (or is it third?) that we had again ventured out on the big water. I had hoped we might use the airboat, which employs an airplane propeller and wind for its speedy propulsion over the shallow water of the marshes, instead of an outboard motor, which frequently stalls in the mud and becomes tangled in the waterweeds. This "machine of the devil" as an English friend described it, was first developed at the Bear River Refuge in Utah to facilitate the gathering of ducks afflicted with botulism. I wanted James to have a ride in one, but it was being repaired.

MAY 7

Roger had promised me a ride in an airboat, but we had to hire an outboard instead. The young man at the engine knew where to find us one of the rarest birds of the United States, the Everglade kite.

The giant snail, *Pomacea caliginosa*, is the staple diet of two birds which could not live in Florida without it—the limpkin and the Everglade kite (or snail kite). It is a huge snail; we found many of its thin discarded shells among the reeds, and on the stems, like clusters of small pearls, were its pinkish-white eggs. It was the other snail bird, the limpkin, that put us on to our first Everglade kites.

One of these extraordinary birds—a kind of compromise between a crane and a water rail—was shrieking, yelping, and caterwauling around a patch of reeds. Apparently they are more vocal just before a storm; thunderheads were threatening in the west. We got to the place where the bird was crying by charging blindly through the marsh. Every now and then our boatman would jump out into the water up to his waist, free the propeller, and give us fifty yards of push into clear water. No sooner had we spotted the noisy limpkin than we saw our first Everglade kite in the distance. The big dark bird sailed lazily along at reed height, then dropped into the reeds and disappeared. We quickly saw another and later a third. We maneuvered slowly to get within binocular distance of the first bird, which had come into view again, perched among the tops of the reeds. These birds can climb about in the reeds like any bittern and in their own way have as much agility in their unusual medium as the limpkin. Our snail kite had found its snail; holding on to a cluster of reeds with one foot and grasping the snail in the other, it carefully picked the animal bit by bit out of its shell by means of its curious slender hooked beak.

The Everglade kite is much wider-winged than any of the other three American kites, more like a harrier, but without the typical action of the harrier. In the air, of course, it has no maneuvering to do, for it is not looking for prey more mobile than snails. This explains, of course, the calm quartering of the reeds by the birds—that slow, low, steady flight, head down, watching the marsh like a black tern. Occasionally they hover on beating wings like an osprey or large kestrel and drop out of sight into the reeds. I do not think they paid much attention to our boat, but I am sure the airboat would have frightened them (Roger says not). One of the birds was certainly a female or a first-year male, rather streaked and not unlike a female harrier. Another was an adult male, quite black except for the white at the base of the tail which both sexes have; at close range bright red legs and bare red skin around its face gave it a most attractive touch of color.

James, with his private passion for seabirds, his diary hinted, was more impressed on this day by the flock of black skimmers which sat on a sandy spit in the lake and dodged his efforts at photography. And for a quarter of an hour he wasted time trying to photograph a very tame least tern that kept returning to a stake marking a boat channel.

I emphasized to him that relatively few American ornithologists have seen the Everglade kite—although our young boatman practically guarantees success to his bird-watching customers. There are probably no more than twenty-five pairs remaining in the United States today—perhaps all of them in this limited area. This puts the species about on a par with the California condor for Number 3 place among rare North American birds; it is anyone's guess which of the two is the rarer. Actually the condor would be the greater loss because it represents a full species, whereas the kite is a local subspecies of a bird that ranges from southern Mexico to the Argentine.

Fifteen years ago Marvin Chandler, the first Audubon warden at Lake Okeechobee, showed me several kite nests in the big glossy-ibis colony, and I had great sport stalking perched birds with my Leica. By wading on my knees, only my head above the tepid water, I could get close enough for some fine shots with the six-inch lens. These I used later in designing a poster which implored duck hunters not to shoot these harmless Raptores. They were distributed by the National Audubon Society and displayed at all fish camps and gun clubs around the lake. Our boatman still had a small supply which he put up wherever he thought they would do the most good.

It is the trigger-happy duck hunter who is the greatest threat to the few remaining kites; they look like any other hawks to him. The unscrupulous egg collector is the next menace, although there are not many active oölogists left in the United States. They are not the problem that they still seem to be in England.*

As late as 1920 there were probably hundreds of Everglade kites still left in Florida. But today the last ones have gone from the St. Johns River and they are no longer found in the Everglades; so the name "snail kite" is now the more appropriate. Marsh drainage did much of the damage. Even temporary drainage eliminates the *Pomacea* snails on which the birds depend. Fortunately, Okeechobee is undrainable; but *raising* the water would be just as bad.

All four North American kites are now far rarer than they were formerly. This afternoon we had seen the rarest of the four, and before the day was out we were also to see the most beautiful one, as James recounts in his diary.

In the little town of Clewiston, with its stately avenues of royal palms and neat houses, we were looking for a bird of exceptional rarity, the smooth-billed ani. An extraordinary, swallow-shaped, graceful hawk came wheeling over us. It had staring white underparts and wing-linings, black wing-ends, black tail-streamers, and when it turned and swung over the casuarina trees, it was black on the upper parts. Its tail was much longer and more deeply forked than that of any other kite. This, the swallow-tailed kite, is common only in the lower Everglades and in a few other swamps in the South. Although it once roamed as far north as Minnesota, Roger tells me we are not likely to see it again after we leave Florida.

It was Jack Merritt of Clewiston who finally showed us the anis. We could not find the little flock at first; we drove up and down the streets looking at every garden, finally to discover them in a field

---

*James might contradict this—we ran into three during our North American journey!

at the edge of town. These close cousins of the cuckoo were quite black and slender, long-tailed, short-winged, and with enormous high-ridged bills; they seemed very loose-jointed. There is another species, the groove-billed ani, which lives in Texas, but with this exception there is nothing else like the bird—although, flying in the distance, it might be mistaken for a grackle. We watched the flock, as the evening fell at Clewiston, assembling at their roosting tree. Until the nineteen-thirties the smooth-billed ani was a vagrant to the United States, but in 1937 a flock, perhaps hurricane-borne from the West Indies, arrived at Miami Beach, where they roosted in an immense clump of bamboo. Since then the bird has bred at more than one place in Florida, though the only regular colony is that at Clewiston; the townspeople are very proud of this ornitho-logical distinction. The birds, as is their custom, nest communally. All the females of the flock lay their eggs in a large nest in more than one layer, with leaves in between. It is probable that the heat and fermentation of the leaves aid in the incubation of the eggs.

While we were watching the anis go to bed, nighthawks hawked for dragonflies over the rooftops and vacant lots of the town. So did a dozen gull-billed terns. It was a bizarre setting for terns. But any-thing seemed possible in this strange part of Florida. And somehow it was difficult to be overwhelmingly surprised by the snail kites and the anis, incredibly rare though they were. By now the incredibly rare was becoming almost commonplace.

Edwin Way Teale

SWALLOW CLOUDS (1956)

THE SEASON OF SUMMER extends to about September 21 but the summer season ends with Labor Day. Then the newspapers begin referring to summer in the past tense. Vacations are over. Schools commence. To the popular mind, September belongs to autumn as December belongs to winter.

This unofficial beginning of the fall lay behind us as we ran down the New Jersey coast, advancing another 250 miles to Cape May and the drowned river of the Delaware estuary. The air was hazy and heavy under the blaze of the morning sun. We crept through the Long Island suburbs, threaded our way among the sweltering canyons of New York, dipped under the Hudson and emerged amid all the villainous smells of that caldron and retort and crucible of the east, the miles and miles of factories west of the river. Then we were out in open country, on U.S. 1, following the same road that had carried us south, on a February day, to begin our travels with the spring.

Now along that road Queen Anne's lace was going to seed, balling up like fingers closing into a fist. Already a few tupelos had turned a deep and winy red. And out of all the grassclumps arose the steely murmur of the insects, the song of autumn that was to accompany us from coast to coast.

By the time we reached the pine barrens of central New Jersey thunderheads had boiled up around the horizon and vultures pitched and banked in a stormy wind. We passed Forked River and

Cedar Run and the purplish, gust-worried water at the mouth of Mullica River under darkening skies. And when, just south of the Mason and Dixon line, we came to old Cape May, the scene of Alexander Wilson's pioneer observations and a mecca for generations of autumn bird watchers, the rain was already a gray curtain over the ocean.

That night the tail end of a hurricane that had headed inland through the Carolinas reached Cape May. We watched the seething white tumult of the surf from an upper room in an old inn facing the sea. All that wild and windy night the rain and spray, the flying foam and driven sand whipped and battered the windowpanes.

We had first looked from those windows nearly fifteen autumns before. Then we were making our initial visit to this far-southern tip of New Jersey, this eighteen-mile point of land thrusting south-southwest with the Atlantic rolling in on one side and the wide Delaware Bay stretching away on the other. Here pirates had once landed to fill their casks with fresh water at Lake Lily. Here, in the heyday of its 150 years as a summer resort, had come Abraham Lincoln and Henry Clay and Horace Greeley and U. S. Grant. Its spacious verandas and lacelike grillwork speak of another age of architecture. Henry Ford, near the turn of the century, had ridden at the wheel of a racing car on the packed sand of its miles of beach. In the swamps of the cape, "cedar mining" had once been a flourishing business with "shingle miners" unearthing blown-down, long buried trees that still contained sound and usable wood. At one time, it is said, Independence Hall in Philadelphia was shingled with cedar mined from the swamps of Cape May.

But to the naturalist Cape May means above all else birds in the autumn. It is one of the great bottlenecks of the Atlantic Coast Flyway. At the tip of the peninsula eleven miles of water extend across Delaware Bay to the high dunes of Cape Henlopen. West across the bay from Cape May Point the distance is twenty miles. To find a crossing of less than eleven miles a bird would have to travel forty miles up the wide Delaware estuary. So, at certain times the migrants, reluctant to venture over the water lest they be driven out to sea by the wind, pile up near the tip of the point in spectacular concentrations. On September 1, 1920, Witmer Stone, author of *Bird Studies at Old Cape May*, counted eighty-six species on a walk along the bay side of the point. Even as late as December 22, the 1935 Christmas census of the Delaware Valley Ornithological Club yielded 111 species. On October 27 of that same year members of a National Audubon Society field trip to the point piled up 123 species. Seventeen years went by before, on September 21, 1952, a party led by Julian K. Potter raised that figure by one to the present record total of 124 species seen in a single day.

While the storm pounded the shingled walls and rattled the windows that night Nellie and I recalled our other visits in the fall to this historic cape. We remembered the time migrating hordes of monarch butterflies embrowned whole branches as they clung to the Spanish oaks within the circle at Cape May Point. We remembered a distant cloud of thousands of sanderlings that appeared and disappeared, flashing like a myriad twinkling lights each time the shorebirds turned and their white underparts caught the sun. We recalled a morning beside Lake Lily when we looked directly up into a revolving wheel of broad-winged hawks, 200 or more circling together, rising higher and higher until the wheel dissolved and all the buteos streamed away toward the distant dunes of Henlopen. We spoke of such things. Recollections of other autumns returned. And as we talked we remembered also a congenial companion on other visits to the cape.

An idea I have encountered from time to time—an idea that no doubt has been carefully nurtured by authors—is the belief that an author is an interesting, exciting person compared to a publisher grubbing among cost sheets, waybills and forms relating to the excess profits tax. The fact is that this companion, Raymond T. Bond, is both a publisher and one of the most complexly interesting men we know. I remember a time when we all started for Cape May late in the afternoon. I had just turned in an index after working night and day and there apparently was some doubt concerning my ability to stay awake at the wheel as we rode hour after hour through the night. But Bondie talked. He talked almost all the way—wonderful recollections so engrossing they kept me wide awake and the car safely on the road.

Who else do we know who ever had a relative who began reading the *Encyclopedia Britannica* from end to end and got through "D" and ever afterwards was amazingly learned in conversation so long as the topics ranged from A to D? Who else ever heard of two unliterary ladies known in their family circle as "The Little-Read Aunts"? Who else ever disconcerted a thug who stepped from behind a tree on a dark street by brushing past with the words: "Sorry, I haven't got a match"? Who else ever had an ancestor who befriended Victor Hugo in exile and was rewarded by appearing in the cast of characters of *Toilers of the Sea*? Or for that matter, being a teetotaler, who else ever had a middle name meaning "Wine Taster"? Certainly no one else ever proved, eruditely and to our satisfaction, that hell is a place where there are no birds by quoting Virgil's famous line from the sixth book of the *Aeneid*: "Easy is the descent to Hell—Facilis descensus Averno." Avernus, Virgil's portal to Hades—a noxious lake in the Italian Campania where fumes were supposed to kill all birds flying overhead—received its name from the Greek *Aornos*, *a* not, and *ornos* or *ornis*, a bird. So it seemed an eminently logical step to Bond, who has been an avid bird watcher since boyhood, that hell should thus be construed to be a place without birds and a place without birds to be hell.

By morning the storm had largely spent itself. The surf was high but the clouds were breaking. September, a month that along the

Middle Atlantic States has fewer days of rain than June, July or August, was reverting to normal. After a quick breakfast in a restaurant where the waitress asked us if we wanted "white or tan bread" we wandered down the side roads of a dripping landscape, into a day of swallow clouds.

By July, each year, the white-breasted tree swallows begin congregating in the coastal marshes of the northeastern states. Their numbers are so great that they sometimes festoon telephone wires, sitting side by side literally for miles on end. Hence a colloquial name: "Wire Birds." Their fall migration, beginning early, is a leisurely drifting down the map. Traveling by day, feeding on the wing, they loiter along the road. If a tree swallow's flight were straightened out it would cover a good many miles in a day. Harold B. Moore, a physician of Harrisburg, Pennsylvania, reported in *The Auk* in the early 1930's that a migrating tree swallow, flying beside his car down a straight road on a windless day, advanced steadily at a speed of twenty-five miles an hour. But most of the time the great flocks of the early swallows pause and advance, move south little by little.

Paradoxically they are one of the first to gather for migration and one of the last to go. In fact some never go. On December 31, the final day of the year, several tree swallows were seen feeding on bayberries and flitting over frozen Lake Lily at Cape May Point. This is the only species of swallow to be reported every week in the year from the New York region. I have sometimes found a hundred or more overwintering among the phragmites and bayberry bushes of the Jones Beach area on the south shore of Long Island.

During late August and early September, especially when the prevailing gentle, southerly breezes are supplemented for a day or so by winds from the northwest, tremendous numbers of tree swallows pile up near the tip of Cape May. This is the first spectacular bird event of fall. Roosting by night among the canebrakes of the phragmites, with as many as four or five swallows clinging to a single reed, and supplementing their insect fare by day with the frosty-gray berries of the wax myrtle or bayberry, they build up the fat that will provide fuel for the later, longer flights of autumn. Not only are birds at their peak in numbers in the fall but they are at their peak in weight. If you could weigh the southbound migrants of an American autumn, you would have more pounds of birds than at any other time of year.

We were heading for the western side of the point—where a concrete ship still lies where it ran aground in World War I and where water-smoothed bits of quartz, "Cape May diamonds," are scattered through the sand—when we came within sight of the first multitude of swallows. Over a wide expanse of open ground they formed a living cloud, acres in extent, continually in motion, continually changing form, swirling this way and that like windblown smoke. The cloud rose and fell. It elongated and contracted. It condensed and grew vaporous. It scudded low across the ground, zoomed as though caught in a violent updraft. Thousands of separate birds were lost in the group movement, lifting, veering, diving, together.

There was something hypnotic, something deeply stirring in the sight. Swarm was the word that came instantly to mind. This teeming cloud of birds not only suggested a swarm of bees but there was something about their wild abandon, their holiday mood, that was akin to the spirit of the honeybees when they leave the hive on the great communal adventure of their lives.

We tried to estimate the number of birds in the moving cloud before us. Perhaps if, like some members of the Linnaean Society in New York, we had trained ourselves by dumping rice grains on a tabletop, estimating the number and then counting them, we might have had better success. As it was we settled for the rather vague term, "many thousands." Without doubt there are oftentimes more than 10,000 white-breasted swallows in one of these Cape May concentrations.

John James Audubon, in the first volume of his *Ornithological Biography*, describes how overwintering tree swallows along the estuaries of the Mississippi in Louisiana flew in dense masses low over the water at dawn. During these flights, he added, numbers of the birds were often killed by canoe men "with the mere aid of their paddles." These beautiful and beneficial swallows at one time were sold for food in the New York market. Alexander Wilson recalls, in his *American Ornithology*, an instance in which a meat-gunner near Cape May fired into a cloud of tree swallows, killing or maiming 102 birds with a single shot. Such slaughter, once familiar to the cape, is now a thing of the past. But even today that ancient, and currently self-righteous, enmity of the human predator for the avian predator persists and every Cape May autumn is still tainted with the senseless slaughter of hawks for sport and so-called food.

The cloud of the swallows drifted away. Later we saw this same concentration again and, driving northward up the cape, at least two other swallow-swarms—one over pastureland, the other above a wide salt meadow where a river entered the sea. All the evolutions on this day were comparatively low in the sky but sometimes a cloud of swallows will ascend up and up until the individual birds are nearly lost to sight. Several times, here and there, we came upon small groups resting and feeding on the bayberry bushes. So voracious are these autumn swallows for the gray, waxy fruit that as many as forty-one bayberries have been found in the digestive system of a single bird.

There were, that day, various other early migrants—redstarts, veeries, sharp-shinned hawks, red-breasted nuthatches. We saw them among the bushes and trees along the roads, near the seventy-foot Cape May Lighthouse and amid the sorry wreckage of the Witmer Stone Wildlife Sanctuary, blighted by chemical dust from the high chimneys of the neighboring magnesite plant. But this was our tree-swallow day. Above all else it was the swallow clouds, the thousands upon thousands of white-breasted, dark-winged birds swirling and scudding in unison, that made this particular one of the traditional "thirty golden days of September" so memorable. The swallows of Cape May formed our outstanding recollection of the Atlantic Coast Flyway, that first of the four great paths of migration down the North American continent.

While we would be working west toward and across the other three, the flood of migrant birds would mount at Old Cape May. Some, like the knots, would follow a narrow lane close to the edge of the sea; others, like the thrushes and kinglets and warblers, would be moving south on a wide advancing front. It is these latter birds that are swept into the long pocket of the cape by northwest winds in the night. Many of them are carried out to sea and lost. Others, when dawn breaks, find themselves still within sight of land and are able to come ashore. I remember one morning when a steady parade of sharp-shinned hawks, hours long, came in from the sea. So numerous were they that we sometimes had half a hundred within sight at the same time.

On another occasion, when a great wind from the northwest was booming over the boardwalk at Cape May on a September night, I came upon a little kinglet fluttering against a lighted window of the Municipal Pier. I caught it, holding it loosely in my hand, and felt the violent pounding of its tiny heart. Suddenly it fluttered; the wind tore it from my grasp; it disappeared in an instant, whirled away across the white surf, out over the tumultuous sea, a small, doomed bird in the midst of a night of terror. In that moment I remembered the many times during these autumn expeditions when I had wished for a wind from the northwest to concentrate birds at Cape May. And I regretted every wish. At such times we see only the survivors. We miss the many small migrants that, helpless in the wind and dark, are carried to death at sea.

Although we found no "Cape May diamonds" along the sandy

western shore of the point, that day, we did glimpse something far more precious, an avian jewel once given up for lost, a bird that was listed half a century ago as totally extirpated in the state, a snowy egret passing overhead in buoyant flight. Another persecuted species at one time familiar here but now long gone is the whooping crane. With hardly more than a score of individuals in the world today, it is making a final stand at the Aransas Wildlife Refuge in southern Texas. Yet hardly more than a hundred years ago it sailed on seven-and-a-half-foot, white, black-tipped wings above this very shore. It fed among the sea meadows and marshes near by. Sometimes it even overwintered in the swamps of the Cape May region.

Ogden Nash

UP FROM THE EGG: THE CONFESSIONS OF A NUTHATCH AVOIDER (1957)

Bird watchers top my honors list.
I aimed to be one, but I missed.
Since I'm both myopic and astigmatic,
My aim turned out to be erratic,
And I, bespectacled and binocular,
Exposed myself to comment jocular.
We don't need too much birdlore, do we,
To tell a flamingo from a towhee;
Yet I cannot, and never will,
Unless the silly birds stand still.
And there's no enlightenment in a tour
Of ornithological literature.
Is yon strange creature a common chickadee,
Or a migrant *alouette* from Picardy?
You rush to consult your Nature guide
And inspect the gallery inside,
But a bird in the open never looks
Like its picture in the birdie books—
Or if it once did, it has changed its plumage,
And plunges you back into ignorant gloomage.
That is why I sit here growing old by inches,
Watching the clock instead of finches,
But I sometimes visualize in my gin
The Audubon that I audubin.

Robinson Jeffers

VULTURE (1963)

I had walked since dawn and lay down to rest on a bare hillside
Above the ocean. I saw through half-shut eyelids a vulture
    wheeling high up in heaven,
And presently it passed again, but lower and nearer, its orbit
    narrowing, I understood then
That I was under inspection. I lay death-still and heard the
    flight-feathers
Whistle above me and make their circle and come nearer. I
    could see the naked red head between the great wings
Beak downward staring. I said "My dear bird we are wasting
    time here.
These old bones will still work; they are not for you." But how
    beautiful he'd looked, gliding down
On those great sails; how beautiful he looked, veering away
    in the sea-light over the precipice. I tell you solemnly
That I was sorry to have disappointed him. To be eaten by
    that beak and become part of him, to share those wings
    and those eyes—
What a sublime end of one's body, what an enskyment; what
    a life after death.

William Carlos Williams

BIRD SONG (1963)

It is May on every hand
when the Towhee sings
to his silent mate

at the bottom of
the garden
flaunting his startling

colors moving restlessly
from one
leafless magnolia twig

to another—
announcing spring is
here spring is here

Elizabeth Bishop

SANDPIPER (1965)

The roaring alongside he takes for granted,
and that every so often the world is bound to shake.
He runs, he runs to the south, finical, awkward,
in a state of controlled panic, a student of Blake.

The beach hisses like fat. On his left, a sheet
of interrupting water comes and goes
and glazes over his dark and brittle feet.
He runs, he runs straight through it, watching his toes.

—Watching, rather, the spaces of sand between them,
where (no detail too small) the Atlantic drains
rapidly backwards and downwards. As he runs,
he stares at the dragging grains.

The world is a mist. The world is uniquely
minute and vast and clear. The tide
is higher or lower. He couldn't tell you which.
His beak is focussed; he is preoccupied,

looking for something, something, something.
Poor bird, he is obsessed!
The millions of grains are black, white, tan, and gray,
mixed with quartz grains, rose and amethyst.

Randall Jarrell

THE MOCKINGBIRD (1965)

Look one way and the sun is going down,
Look the other and the moon is rising.
The sparrow's shadow's longer than the lawn.
The bats squeak: "Night is here"; the birds cheep:
   "Day is gone."
On the willow's highest branch, monopolizing
Day and night, cheeping, squeaking, soaring,
The mockingbird is imitating life.

All day the mockingbird has owned the yard.
As light first woke the world, the sparrows trooped
Onto the seedy lawn: the mockingbird
Chased them off shrieking. Hour by hour, fighting hard
To make the world his own, he swooped
On thrushes, thrashers, jays, and chickadees—
At noon he drove away a big black cat.

Now, in the moonlight, he sits here and sings.
A thrush is singing, then a thrasher, then a jay—
Then, all at once, a cat begins meowing.
A mockingbird can sound like anything.
He imitates the world he drove away
So well that for a minute, in the moonlight,
Which one's the mockingbird? which one's the world?

John Haines

IF THE OWL CALLS AGAIN (1966)

at dusk
from the island in the river,
and it's not too cold,

I'll wait for the moon
to rise,
then take wing and glide
to meet him.

We will not speak,
but hooded against the frost
soar above
the alder flats, searching
with tawny eyes.

And then we'll sit
in the shadowy spruce
and pick the bones
of careless mice,

while the long moon drifts
toward Asia
and the river mutters
in its icy bed.

And when the morning climbs
the limbs
we'll part without a sound,

fulfilled, floating
homeward as
the cold world awakens.

John Hollander

SWAN AND SHADOW (1968)

```
                    Dusk
                 Above the
         water   hang   the
                    loud
                    flies
                   Here
                   O so
                   gray
                   then
                  What                        A pale signal will appear
                  When                    Soon before its shadow fades
                  Where                   Here in this pool of opened eye
                  In us          No Upon us As at the very edges
                   of where we take shape in the dark air
                     this object bares its image awakening
                       ripples of recognition that will
                         brush darkness up into light
even after this bird this hour both drift by atop the perfect sad instant now
                          already passing out of sight
                        toward yet-untroubled reflection
                      this image bears its object darkening
                     into memorial shades Scattered bits of
                  light       No of water Or something across
                  water             Breaking up No Being regathered
                  soon                 Yet by then a swan will have
                  gone                    Yes out of mind into what
                   vast
                   pale
                   hush
                   of a
                  place
                   past
        sudden   dark   as
                 if a swan
                   sang
```

William Stafford

JUNCOS (1973)

They operate from elsewhere,
some hall in the mountains—
quick visit, gone.
Specialists on branch ends,
craft union. I like their
clean little coveralls.

Gary Snyder

MAGPIE'S SONG (1974)

Six A.M.,
Sat down on excavation gravel
by juniper and desert S.P. tracks
interstate 80 not far off
        between trucks
Coyotes—maybe three
                howling and yapping from a rise.

Magpie on a bough
Tipped his head and said,

> *"Here in the mind, brother*
> *Turquoise blue.*
> *I wouldn't fool you.*
> *Smell the breeze*
> *It came through all the trees*
> *No need to fear*
> *What's ahead*
> *Snow up on the hills west*
> *Will be there every year*
> *be at rest.*
> *A feather on the ground—*
> *The wind sound—*

Here in the Mind, Brother,
Turquoise Blue"

Barry Lopez

THE RAVEN (1976)

I AM GOING TO have to start at the other end by telling you this: there are no crows in the desert. What appear to be crows are ravens. You must examine the crow, however, before you can understand the raven. To forget the crow completely, as some have tried to do, would be like trying to understand the one who stayed without talking to the one who left. It is important to make note of who has left the desert.

To begin with, the crow does nothing alone. He cannot abide silence and he is prone to stealing things, twigs and bits of straw, from the nests of his neighbors. It is a game with him. He enjoys tricks. If he cannot make up his mind the crow will take two or three wives, but this is not a game. The crow is very accommodating and he admires compulsiveness.

Crows will live in street trees in the residential areas of great cities. They will walk at night on the roofs of parked cars and peck at the grit; they will scrape the pinpoints of their talons across the steel and, with their necks outthrust, watch for frightened children listening in their beds.

Put all this to the raven: he will open his mouth as if to say something. Then he will look the other way and say nothing. Later, when you have forgotten, he will tell you he admires the crow.

The raven is larger than the crow and has a beard of black feathers at his throat. He is careful to kill only what he needs. Crows, on the other hand, will search out the great horned owl, kick and punch him awake, and then, for roosting too close to their nests, they will kill him. They will come out of the sky on a fat, hot afternoon and slam into the head of a dozing rabbit and go away laughing. They will tear out a whole row of planted corn and eat only a few kernels. They will defecate on scarecrows and go home and sleep with 200,000 of their friends in an atmosphere of congratulation. Again, it is only a game; this should not be taken to mean that they are evil.

There is however this: when too many crows come together on a roost there is a lot of shoving and noise and a white film begins to descend over the crows' eyes and they go blind. They fall from their perches and lie on the ground and starve to death. When confronted with this information, crows will look past you and warn you vacantly that it is easy to be misled.

The crow flies like a pigeon. The raven flies like a hawk. He is seen only at a great distance and then not very clearly. This is true of the crow too, but if you are very clever you can trap the crow. The only way to be sure what you have seen is a raven is to follow him until he dies of old age, and then examine the body.

Once there were many crows in the desert. I am told it was like this: you could sit back in the rocks and watch a pack of crows working over the carcass of a coyote. Some would eat, the others would try to squeeze out the vultures. The raven would never be seen. He would be at a distance, alone, perhaps eating a scorpion.

There was, at this time, a small alkaline water hole at the desert's edge. Its waters were bitter. No one but crows would drink there, although they drank sparingly, just one or two sips at a time. One day a raven warned someone about the dangers of drinking the bitter water and was overheard by a crow. When word of this passed among the crows they felt insulted. They jeered and raised insulting gestures to the ravens. They bullied each other into drinking the alkaline water until they had drunk the hole dry and gone blind.

The crows flew into canyon walls and dove straight into the

ground at forty miles an hour and broke their necks. The worst of it was their cartwheeling across the desert floor, stiff wings outstretched, beaks agape, white eyes ballooning, surprising rattlesnakes hidden under sage bushes out of the noonday sun. The snakes awoke, struck and held. The wheeling birds strew them across the desert like sprung traps.

When all the crows were finally dead, the desert bacteria and fungi bored into them, burrowed through bone and muscle, through aqueous humor and feathers until they had reduced the stiff limbs of soft black to blue dust.

After that, there were no more crows in the desert. The few who watched from a distance took it as a sign and moved away.

Finally there is this: one morning four ravens sat at the edge of the desert waiting for the sun to rise. They had been there all night and the dew was like beads of quicksilver on their wings. Their eyes were closed and they were as still as the cracks in the desert floor.

The wind came off the snow-capped peaks to the north and ruffled their breath feathers. Their talons arched in the white earth and they smoothed their wings with sleek, dark bills. At first light their bodies swelled and their eyes flashed purple. When the dew dried on their wings they lifted off from the desert floor and flew away in four directions. Crows would never have had the patience for this.

If you want to know more about the raven: bury yourself in the desert so that you have a commanding view of the high basalt cliffs where he lives. Let only your eyes protrude. Do not blink—the movement will alert the raven to your continued presence. Wait until a generation of ravens has passed away. Of the new generation there will be at least one bird who will find you. He will see your eyes staring up out of the desert floor. The raven is cautious, but he is thorough. He will sense your peaceful intentions. Let him have the first word. Be careful: he will tell you he knows nothing.

If you do not have the time for this, scour the weathered desert shacks for some sign of the raven's body. Look under old mattresses and beneath loose floorboards. Look behind the walls. Sooner or later you will find a severed foot. It will be his and it will be well preserved.

Take it out in the sunlight and examine it closely. Notice that there are three fingers that face forward, and a fourth, the longest and like a thumb, that faces to the rear. The instrument will be black but no longer shiny, the back of it sheathed in armor plate and the underside padded like a wolf's foot.

At the end of each digit you will find a black, curved talon. You will see that the talons are not as sharp as you might have suspected. They are made to grasp and hold fast, not to puncture. They are more like the jaws of a trap than a fistful of ice picks. The subtle difference serves the raven well in the desert. He can weather a storm on a barren juniper limb; he can pick up and examine the crow's eye without breaking it.

Anthony Hecht

HOUSE SPARROWS (1979)

Not of the wealthy, Coral Gables class
Of travelers, nor that rarified tax bracket,
These birds weathered the brutal, wind-chill facts
Under our eaves, nesting in withered grass,
Wormless but hopeful, and now their voice enacts
Forsythian spring with primavernal racket.

Their color is the elderly, moleskin gray
Of doggedness, of mist, magnolia bark.
Salt of the earth, they are; the common clay;
Meek *émigrés* come over on the Ark
In steerage from the Old Country of the Drowned
To settle down along Long Island Sound,

Flatbush, Weehawken, our brownstone tenements,
Wherever the local idiom is *Cheep.*
Savers of string, meticulous and mild,
They are given to nervous flight, the troubled sleep
Of those who remember terrible events,
The wide-eyed, anxious haste of the exiled.

Like all the poor, their safety lies in numbers
And hardihood and anonymity
In a world of dripping browns and duns and umbers.

They have inherited the lower sky,
Their Lake of Constants, their blue modality
That they are borne upon and battered by.

Those little shin-bones, hollow at the core,
Emaciate finger-joints, those fleshless wrists,
Wrapped in a wrinkled, loose, rice-paper skin,
As though the harvests of earth had never been,
Where have we seen such frailty before?
In pictures of Biafra and Auschwitz.

Yet here they are, these chipper stratoliners,
Unsullen, unresentful, full of the grace
Of cheerfulness, who seem to greet all comers
With the wild confidence of Forty-Niners,
And, to the lively honor of their race,
Rude canticles of "Summers, Summers, Summers."

Sterling A. Brown

IDYLL (1980)

I found me a cranny of perpetual dusk.
There for the grateful sense was pungent musk
Of rotting leaves, and moss, mingled with scents
Of heavy clusters freighting foxgrape vines.
The sun was barred except at close of day
When he could weakly etch in changing lines
A filigree upon the silver trunks
Of maple and of poplar. There were oaks
Their black bark fungus-spotted, and there lay
An old wormeaten segment of gray fence
Tumbling in consonant long forgot decay.
Motionless the place save when a little wind
Rippled the leaves, and soundless too it was
Save for a stream nearly inaudible,
That made a short stay in closewoven grass
Then in elusive whispers bade farewell;
Save for the noise of birds, whistling security.

One afternoon I lay there drowsily
Steeped in the crannies' love benevolence;
Peaceful the far dreams I was dreaming of. . . .
Sharply a stranger whistle screeched above
Once then again. Nearly as suddenly
A hawk dove, swooping past the sagging fence

Past a short shrub, and like a heavy rock
Striking the ground. I started up, the hawk
Flew off unhurriedly with fine insolence,
On vigorous wings, and settled on the limb
Of a dead chestnut. His sentinel mate
Screeched down another cry, almost too late.

On the matting of the leaves, a small bird lay
Spattering blood and on the little stream
A fluff of blue feathers floated away.
The hawk awhile gazed at me, I at him—
Splendid the corsair's breast and head of white
And dauntless, daring poise. Then with a cry
Frustrate, vindictive, he wheeled in graceful flight.
The wind stirred faintly, there was nothing more
Of sound, except a snatch of woodland song
As earlier. The stream purred listlessly along,
And all grew quite as peaceful as before.

Faith McNulty

THE EVER HUNGRY JAY (1980)

IN THE WINTER we who live in the country owe a great debt to the birds that consent to come to our bird feeders. Everyone I know has a bird feeder and the action at the feeder is a major source of interest and conversation. Bird-feeding people employ various methods and devices. They have favorite birds and less favorite birds. The differing devices are feeders cleverly designed to let some birds get at the seed and exclude others. The bird most people want to exclude is the blue jay. A blue jay will sit in a bird feeder and swallow one sunflower seed after another as though his stomach were a bottomless pit. He swallows conspicuously. You can see the seed go down and hit bottom—thunk!—and then he gobbles another. While eating he looks rude and complacent—elbows on the table, no suggestion of gratitude. Sunflower seed is the blue jay's special delight—as it is for almost all birds—and it is the most expensive seed commonly fed to birds. I've heard people say they simply couldn't afford to be ripped off by blue jays and so they have bought elaborate contraptions to thwart them. Snowbound and watching birds wistfully, wishing I could sail over the white meadows instead of floundering, I began to think about the economics of bird feeding and social attitudes; to wonder if there is any parallel with some other public charities—a tendency to exclude some welfare cases on grounds of their ingratitude, lack of real need, or high cost, while we spend even more money to weed them out of the system. I decided to do a little local research with a view to answering such questions as these: Is the blue jay needy or greedy? Is it possible to fill up a blue jay? Do they have other resources, as some of my friends suspect, and simply prefer handouts? What is the cost of sunflower seed and how does this cost relate to the cost of a blue-jay-excluding device?

At the time of my investigation Damon's Hardware in Wakefield, Rhode Island, was selling twelve and a half pounds of sunflower seed for $4.50 and fifty pounds for $14.95. I took ten seeds to the drugstore and had them weighed on an apothecary's scale. With the help of my husband I computed that ten seeds weighing .92 grams equal 3/100 of an ounce. At this rate there are 4,969 seeds to the pound. At $14.95 for fifty pounds, a pound costs about thirty cents. Therefore each seed costs 6/1000 of a cent. In other words, I was able to buy 166 sunflower seeds for a penny.

Mr. Damon told me he sells only the best sunflower seed. They are fat and gray with a white stripe. Small, black sunflower seeds are cheaper, but have less meat. Most sunflower seed is grown, not in Kansas, but in North Dakota, and is a big business. For some reason the seed can't be harvested until after a frost, usually in November, so the seed on the market in October is last year's seed and Damon warns against it. Over the summer worms have hatched and eaten out the hearts. "This old inferior stuff is peddled," he said, "and you have to watch out. Also seed dries out. A bag that weighs fifty pounds in November weighs forty by summer."

Damon showed me his assorted bird feeders. One that is effective against jays has a plastic dome that can be lowered over the feeding tray to make the aperture so small a jay can't perch or get his head in. Another clever one has a counterbalance that works like a see-saw. If a heavy bird sits on the perch it sinks down, snapping shut a strip of metal across the feeding aperture. Since the feeder has a glass front the frustrated bird finds itself sitting there looking at the goodies inside.

While Damon and I were talking, a sunflower seed customer came in and bought four fifty-pound bags. Damon said this was this customer's second two-hundred-pound purchase this year. I asked the man if he excluded jays from his feeder. "They eat like hogs," he said, shouldering a bag, "but they've got to eat, too. I have a feeder just for small birds and feed the jays on the ground."

At home I telephoned a few friends for their views on bird feeding. I am happy to report that everyone I spoke to took a generous and liberal view of jays.

Elisabeth Keiffer, Ministerial Road: "Anyone can come to my feeder. We have no blue jay baffles. I have never understood this discrimination. Grosbeaks are just as fat and greedy but they're very popular."

Rita Lepper, Cherry Road: "We like blue jays. However, we have tried vainly to outfox squirrels. We hung a coconut from a very fine wire, but we have a squirrel who can hang by one toenail and get in."

William Innis, Rose Hill Road: "I think blue jays are very pushy, forward creatures, but I don't hate them. My favorite birds are chickadees and titmice."

Duncan Briggs, Old Post Road: "I have a feeder that keeps blue jays out, but I give them cracked corn on the ground. What the hell, I feed everything. I like nuthatches very much and I like chickadees. They do a terrific job hammering open those seeds."

Carol Mariner, Matunuck: "Don't ask about my bill. It's too awful. I like all the birds . . . everything but evening grosbeaks—they're so disagreeable to each other—and starlings, which are greasy, revolting birds that will eat anything. Blue jays I don't mind. I have a counterweighted feeder, but it doesn't have a glass front. I think that that kind of device is torture. If you're going to feed birds you should do it in a kind way. For a while I had a cage type of feeder with wire mesh that small birds could get through and big ones couldn't. It had a wooden plug in the top. A red squirrel chewed through and got in. Then he ate so much he was too fat to get out. We just had to wait—he and I—for him to get thin. I put in water, as I felt he might get quite dry. It took him forty-eight hours to shrink sufficiently. It was nerve-racking for us both."

C. DeWolf Gibson, Matunuck: "Blue jays are robbers! Absolute robbers! And they squawk a lot. But somehow I admire them just the same." Virginia Kittredge, Ministerial Road: "I adore blue jays. When a blue jay and a cardinal arrive together it's the most thrilling sight of winter." Betty Salomon, Bradford: "Blue jays pay their way. They warn me when something is going on. Sometimes it's a cat at the feeder. The other day the jays made a racket. I went out and saw a sharp-shinned hawk circling overhead. I said, "Thanks, jays, for letting me know." Barbara Davis, Matunuck: "I love blue jays. The bad birds we have are grackles. In the autumn they try to get in the house. They cluster on the sills and peer in at us. My grandmother hated them, too. At the age of eighty she picked up an old shotgun and fired into an apple tree and seven starlings fell dead. She was very pleased."

Having sampled local opinion, I telephoned Lee Gardener, the resident biologist at the Norman Bird Sanctuary in Middletown, Rhode Island, an expert witness on the habits of the blue jay. Members of the family Corvidae, jays are related to crows and are indeed smart and aggressive. They will even attack a person in defense of their young. "I've had a jay swoop and rake my head with its claws when I picked a baby up off the ground. They can lick almost any other bird except a mockingbird, which is even tougher. They live just about everywhere east of the Mississippi. It is hard to count them in a locality. They are casually migratory and move here and there with wind and weather. Their flocks are not due to comradeship but because when one jay finds food others follow, so a group will descend first on one bird feeder and then on another."

Gardener then confirmed the suspicion that blue jays are among the least needy of all the species in the bird breadline. "They are omnivorous and if seeds fail they can go to the beach and eat a clam or to the dump and eat a dead rat," Gardener said. I asked about their conspicuous gobbling, and he explained that, like crows, jays are hiders. They fill their crop with seeds, carry them away, and then cough them up. They husk and eat what they want and hide the rest under leaves or in nooks and crannies. Ecologically it is a valuable trait since jays plant seeds that they forget to dig up and thus help to start new growth, but the habit is indeed quite depleting to the sunflower seed supply at bird feeders. Gardener dismissed as unimportant the competition between jays and smaller birds at feeders, provided the seed supply is ample. If there is enough to go around, the small birds simply sit and wait their turn. Thus an alternative to the blue jay baffler is a sufficient supply of seed.

Gardener's information led me back to my financial calculations. After a half hour of watching jays swallow sunflower seeds, I arrived at a maximum of twenty-five seeds in one sitting. A jay flying away with twenty-five seeds is carrying off 15/100 of a penny's worth. A flock of ten jays is making off with one and a half cents' worth. If they do this three times a day, the cost is four and a half cents. Let's be generous and give them a nickel a day. I am happy that I have come upon this information. As I sit here by my window, aware that if I go out in the tempting, treacherous snow my feet will feel heavy and cold in no time, it is a great vicarious pleasure to watch a jay drift effortlessly from branch to branch—and thence to my offering of sunflower seeds, spread out on an open feeder available to all. I can watch him gobble his twenty-five-seed capacity with an easy mind. At 15/100 of a penny the sight is a real bargain. It gives me a feeling that is rare these days. It makes me feel terribly rich.

Lorna Dee Cervantes

EMPLUMADA (1981)

When summer ended
the leaves of snapdragons withered
taking their shrill-colored mouths with them.
They were still, so quiet. They were
violet where umber now is. She hated
and she hated to see
them go. Flowers

born when the weather was good—this
she thinks of, watching the branch of peaches
daring their ways above the fence, and further,
two hummingbirds, hovering, stuck to each other,
arcing their bodies in grim determination
to find what is good, what is
given them to find. These are warriors

distancing themselves from history.
They find peace
in the way they contain the wind
and are gone.

Robert Penn Warren

REDWING BLACKBIRDS (1981)

How far a-winging to keep this appointment with April!
How much breath left in reserve to fill
The sky of washed azure and whipped-cream cumuli
With their rusty, musical, heart-plumbing cry!

On sedge, winter-bit but erect, on old cattails, they swing.
Throats throb, your field glasses say, as they cling and sing—
If singing is what you call that rusty, gut-grabbing cry
That calls on life to be lived gladly, gladly.

They twist, tumble, tangle, they glide and curvet,
And sun stabs the red splash to scarlet on each epaulet,
And the lazy distance of hills seems to take
A glint more green, and dry grass at your feet to wake.

In the vast of night, seasons later, sleet coding on pane,
Fire dead on hearth, hope banked in heart, I again
Awake, not in dream but with eyes shut, believing I hear
That rusty music far off, far off, and catch flash and fleer

Of a scarlet slash accenting the glossy black. Sleet
Continues. The heart continues its steady beat
As I burrow into the tumulus of sleep,

Where all things are buried, though no man for sure knows
how deep.

The globe grinds on, proceeds with the business of Aprils
and men.
Next year will redwings see me, or I them, again then?
If not, some man else may pause, awaiting that rusty, musical
cry,
And catch—how gallant—the flash of epaulets scarlet against
blue sky.

E. B. White

A LISTENER'S GUIDE TO THE BIRDS (1981)

(After a Binge with Roger Tory Peterson in His Famous Guidebook)

Wouldst know the lark?
Then hark!
Each natural bird
Must be seen *and* heard.
The lark's "Tee-ee" is a tinkling entreaty,
But it's not always "Tee-ee"—
Sometimes it's "Tee-titi."
    So watch yourself.

Birds have their love-and-mating song,
Their warning cry, their hating song;
Some have a night song, some a day song,
A lilt, a tilt, a come-what-may song;
Birds have their careless bough and teeter song
And, of course, their Roger Tory Peter song.

The studious ovenbird (pale pinkish legs)
Calls, "Teacher, teacher, teacher!"
The chestnut-sided warbler begs
To see Miss Beecher.
    "I wish to see Miss Beecher."
(Sometimes interpreted as "Please please please ta meetcha.")

The redwing (frequents swamps and marshes)
Gurgles, "Konk-la-reeee,"
Eliciting from the wood duck
The exclamation "Jeeee!"
    (But that's the *male* wood duck, remember.
    If it's his wife you seek,
    Wait till you hear a distressed "Whoo-eek!")

Nothing is simpler than telling a barn owl from a veery:
One says, "Kschh!" in a voice that is eerie,
The other says, "Vee-ur," in a manner that is breezy.
    (I told you it was easy.)
On the other hand, distinguishing between the veery
And the olive-backed thrush
Is another matter. It couldn't be worse.
The thrush's song is similar to the veery's,
Only it's in reverse.

Let us suppose you hear a bird say, "Fitz-bew,"
The things you can be sure of are two:
First, the bird is an alder flycatcher (*Empidonax traillii traillii*);
Second, you are standing in Ohio—or, as some people call it,
    O-hee-o—
Because, although it may come as a surprise to you,
The alder flycatcher, in New York or New England, does not
    say, "Fitz-bew,"
It says, "Wee-bé-o."

"Chu-chu-chu" is the note of the harrier,
Copied, of course, from our common carrier.
The osprey, thanks to a lucky fluke,
Avoids "Chu-chu" and cries, "Chewk, chewk!"
    So there's no difficulty there.

The chickadee likes to pronounce his name;
It's extremely helpful and adds to his fame.
But in spring you can get the heebie-jeebies
Untangling chickadees from phoebes.
The chickadee, when he's all afire,
Whistles, "Fee-bee," to express desire.
He should be arrested and thrown in jail
For impersonating another male.
    (There's a way you can tell which bird is which,
      But just the same, it's a nasty switch.)
Our gay deceiver may fancy-free be
But he never does fool a female phoebe.

Oh, sweet the random sounds of birds!
The old-squaw, practicing his thirds;
The distant bittern, driving stakes,
The lonely loon on haunted lakes;
The white-throat's pure and tenuous thread—
They go to my heart, they go to my head.
How hard it is to find the words
With which to sing the praise of birds!
Yet birds, when *they* get singing praises,
Don't lack for words—they know some daisies:
    "Fitz-bew,"
    "Konk-la-reeee,"
    "Hip-three-cheers,"
    "Onk-a-lik, ow-owdle-ow,"
    "Cheedle cheedle chew,"
And dozens of other inspired phrases.

        —E. B. WHITE (gray cheeks,
                inconspicuous eye-ring;
                frequents bars and glades)

Robert Creeley

THE BIRDS (1982)

I'll miss the small birds that come
for the sugar you put out
and the bread crumbs. They've

made the edge of the sea domestic
and, as I am, I welcome that.
Nights my head seemed twisted

with dreams and the sea wash,
I let it all come quiet, waking,
counting familiar thoughts and objects.

Here to rest, like they say, I best
liked walking along the beach
past the town till one reached

the other one, around the corner
of rock and small trees. It was
clear, and often empty, and

peaceful. Those lovely ungainly
pelicans fished there, dropping
like rocks, with grace, from the air,

headfirst, then sat on the water,
letting the pouch of their beaks
grow thin again, then swallowing

whatever they'd caught. The birds,
no matter they're not of our kind,
seem most like us here. I want

to go where they go, in a way, if
a small and common one. I want
to ride that air which makes the sea

seem down there, not the element
in which one thrashes to come up.
I love water, I *love* water—

but I also love air, and fire.

Charles Simic

THE GREAT HORNED OWL (1982)

One morning the Grand Seigneur
Is so good as to appear.
He sits in a scrawny little tree
In my backyard.

When I say his name aloud,
He turns his head
And looks at me
In utter disbelief.

I show him my belt,
How I had to
Tighten it lately
To the final hole.

He ruffles his feathers,
Studies the empty woodshed,
The old red Chevy on blocks.
Alas! He's got to be going.

Cornelius Eady

CROWS IN A STRONG WIND (1986)

Off go the crows from the roof.
The crows can't hold on.
They might as well
Be perched on an oil slick.

Such an awkward dance,
These gentlemen
In their spottled-black coats.
Such a tipsy dance,

As if they didn't know where they were.
Such a humorous dance,
As they try to set things right,
As the wind reduces them.

Such a sorrowful dance.
How embarrassing is love
When it goes wrong

In front of everyone.

David Wagoner

KINGFISHER (1987)

The blunt big slate-blue dashing cockaded head
Cocked and the tapering thick of the bill
Sidelong for a black eye staring down
From the elm branch over the pool now poised
Exactly for this immediate moment diving
In a single wingflap wingfold plunging
Slapwash not quite all the way under
The swirling water and upward instantly
In a swerving spiral back to the good branch
With a fingerling catfish before the ripples
Have reached me sitting nearby to follow it
With a flip of a shake from crestfeathers to white
Bibchoker down the crawhatch suddenly
Seeing me and swooping away cackling
From the belt streaked rusty over the full belly.

May Swenson

WATERBIRD (1987)

Part otter, part snake, part bird the bird Anhinga,
jalousie wings, draped open, dry. When slack-
hinged, the wind flips them shut. Her cry,
a slatted clatter, inflates her chin-
pouch; it's like a fish's swim-
bladder. Anhinga's body, otter-
furry, floats, under water-
mosses, neck a snake with white-
rimmed blue round roving eyes. Those long feet stilt-
paddle the only bird of the marsh that flies
submerged. Otter-
quick over bream that hover in water-
shade, she feeds, finds fillets among the waterweeds. Her beak, ferrule of a folded black
umbrella, with neat thrust impales her prey.
She flaps up to dry on the crooked, look-
dead-limb of the Gumbo Limbo, her tan-
tipped wing fans spread, tail a shut fan dangled.

Duane Niatum

SNOWY OWL NEAR OCEAN SHORES (1991)

sits on a stump in an abandoned farmer's field,
a castaway from an arctic tundra storm.
Beyond the dunes cattails toss and bend as snappy
as the surf, rushing and crashing down the jetty.

His head glances round; his eyes, a deeper yellow
than the winter sun, seem to spot a mouse
crawl from a mud hole to bear grass-patch.
When an hour of wind and sleet passes and nothing
darts like the river underground, a North Pole
creature shows us how to last.

The wind ruffles his feathers from crown to claws
while he gazes at the salt-slick rain.
So when a double-rainbow arced the sky
we left him to his white refrain.

Terry Tempest Williams

PEREGRINE FALCON (1991)

lake level: 4205.40'

Not far from Great Salt Lake is the municipal dump. Acres of trash heaped high. Depending on your frame of mind, it is either an olfactory fright show or a sociological gold mine. Either way, it is best to visit in winter.

For the past few years, when the Christmas Bird Count comes around, I seem to be relegated to the landfill. The local Audubon hierarchy tell me I am sent there because I know gulls. The truth lies deeper. It's an under-the-table favor. I am sent to the dump because secretly they know I like it.

As far as birding goes, there's often no place better. Our urban wastelands are becoming wildlife's last stand. The great frontier. We've moved them out of town like all other "low-income tenants."

The dump where I count birds for Christmas used to have cat-tails—but I can't remember them. A few have popped up below the hill again, in spite of the bulldozers, providing critical cover for coots, mallards, and a variety of other waterfowl. I've seen herons standing by and once a snowy egret, but for the most part, the habitat now is garbage, perfect for starlings and gulls.

I like to sit on the piles of unbroken Hefties, black bubbles of sanitation. It provides comfort with a view. Thousands of starlings cover refuse with their feet. Everywhere I look—feathered trash.

The starlings gorge themselves, bumping into each other like drunks. They are not discretionary. They'll eat anything, just like us. Three starlings picked a turkey carcass clean. Afterward, they crawled inside and wore it as a helmet. A carcass with six legs walking around—you have to be sharp counting birds at the dump.

I admire starlings' remarkable adaptability. Home is everywhere. I've seen them nesting under awnings on New York's Fifth Avenue, as well as inside aspen trunks in the Teton wilderness. Over 50 percent of their diet is insects. They are the most effective predators against the clover weevil in America.

Starlings are also quite beautiful if looked at with beginner's eyes. In autumn and winter, their plumage appears speckled, unkempt. But by spring, the lighter tips of their feathers have been worn away, leaving them with a black, glossy plumage, glistening with iridescences.

Inevitably, students at the museum will describe an elegant, black bird with flashes of green, pink, and purple.

"About this big," they say (holding their hands about seven inches apart vertically). "With a bright yellow bill. What is it?"

"A starling," I answer.

What follows is a dejected look flushed with embarrassment.

"Is that all?"

The name precedes the bird.

I understand it. When I'm out at the dump with starlings, I don't want to like them. They are common. They are aggressive, and they behave poorly, crowding out other birds. When a harrier happens to cross-over from the marsh, they swarm him. He disappears. They want their trash to themselves.

Perhaps we project on to starlings that which we deplore in ourselves: our numbers, our aggression, our greed, and our cruelty. Like starlings, we are taking over the world.

The parallels continue. Starlings forage by day in open country competing with native species such as bluebirds for food. They drive them out. In late afternoon, they return in small groups to nest elsewhere, competing with cavity nesters such as flickers, martins, tree swallows, and chickadees. Once again, they move in on other birds' territories.

Starlings are sophisticated mimics singing songs of bobwhites, killdeer, flickers, and phoebes. Their flocks drape bare branches in spring with choruses of chatters, creeks, and coos. Like any good impostor, they confuse the boundaries. They lie.

What is the impact of such a species on the land? Quite simply, a loss of diversity.

What makes our relationship to starlings even more curious is that we loathe them, calling in exterminators because we fear disease, yet we do everything within our power to encourage them as we systematically erase the specialized habitats of specialized birds. I have yet to see a snowy egret spearing a bagel.

The man who wanted Shakespeare's birds flying in Central Park and altruistically brought starlings to America from England, is not to blame. We are—for creating more and more habitat for a bird we despise. Perhaps the only value in the multitudes of starlings we have garnished is that in some small way they allow us to comprehend what vast flocks of birds must have felt like.

The symmetry of starling flocks takes my breath away, I lose track of time and space. At the dump, all it takes is the sweep of my hand. They rise. Hundreds of starlings. They wheel and turn, twist and glide, with no apparent leader. They are the collective. A flight of frenzy. They are black stars against a blue sky. I watch them above the dump, expanding and contracting along the meridian of a winged universe.

Suddenly, the flock pulls together like a winced eye, then opens in an explosion of feathers. A peregrine falcon is expelled, but not without its prey. With folded wings he strikes a starling and plucks its body from mid-air. The flock blinks again and the starlings disperse, one by one, returning to the landfill.

The starlings at the Salt Lake City municipal dump give us numbers that look good on our Christmas Bird Count, thousands, but they become faceless when compared to one peregrine falcon. A century ago, he would have seized a teal.

I will continue to count birds at the dump, hoping for under-the-table favors, but don't mistake my motives. I am not contemplating starlings. It is the falcon I wait for—the duckhawk with a memory for birds that once blotted out the sun.

Mary Oliver

GANNETS (1992)

I am watching the white gannets
blaze down into the water
with the power of blunt spears
and a stunning accuracy—
even though the sea is riled and boiling
and gray with fog
and the fish
are nowhere to be seen,
they fall, they explode into the water
like white gloves,
then they vanish,
then they climb out again,
from the cliff of the wave,
like white flowers—
and still I think
that nothing in this world moves
but as a positive power—
even the fish, finning down into the current
or collapsing
in the red purse of the beak,
are only interrupted from their own pursuit
of whatever it is
that fills their bellies—
and I say:

life is real,

and pain is real,

but death is an imposter,

and if I could be what once I was,

like the wolf or the bear

standing on the cold shore,

I would still see it—

how the fish simply escape, this time,

or how they slide down into a black fire

for a moment,

then rise from the water inseparable

from the gannets' wings.

Linda Hogan

CROW LAW (1993)

The temple where crow worships
walks forward in tall, black grass.
Betrayal is crow's way of saying grace
to the wolf
so it can eat
what is left
when blood is on the ground,
until what remains of moose
is crow
walking out
the sacred temple of ribs
in a dance of leaving
the red tracks of scarce and private gods.
It is the oldest war
where moose becomes wolf and crow,
where the road ceases
to become the old forest
where crow is calling,
where we are still afraid.

Amy Clampitt

SHOREBIRD-WATCHING (1994)

To more than give names
to these random arrivals—
teeterings and dawdlings
of dunlin and turnstone,
black-bellied or golden
plover, all bound for

what may be construed as
a kind of avian Althing
out on the Thingstead,
the unroofed synagogue
of the tundra—is already
to have begun to go wrong.

What calculus, what
tuning, what unparsed
telemetry within the
retina, what overdrive
of hunger for the nightlong
daylight of the arctic,

are we voyeurs of? Our
bearings gone, we fumble
a welter of appearance,

of seasonal plumages
that go dim in winter:
these bright backs'

tweeded saffron, dark
underparts the relic
of what sibylline
descents, what harrowings?
Idiot savants, we've
brought into focus

such constellations,
such gamuts of
errantry, the very
terms we're condemned
to try to think in
turn into a trespass.

But Adam, drawn toward
that dark underside,
its mesmerizing
circumstantial thumbprint,
would already have
been aware of this.

Robert Wrigley

RAVENS AT DEER CREEK (1998)

Something's dead in that stand of fir
one ridge over. Ravens circle and swoop
above the trees, while others
swirl up from below, like paper scraps
blackened in a fire. In the mountains
in winter, it's true: death is a joyful flame,
those caws and cartwheels pure celebration.
It is a long, snowy mile I've come
to see this, thanks to dumb luck or grace.
I meant only a hard ski through powder,
my pulse in my ears, and sweat, the pace
like a mainspring, my breath louder and louder
until I stopped, body an engine
ticking to be cool. And now the birds.
I watch them and think, maybe I have seen
these very ones, speaking without words,
clear-eyed and clerical, ironic, peering in at me
from the berm of snow outside my window,
where I sprinkled a few crumbs of bread. We
are neighbors in the neighborhood of silence.
They've accepted my crumbs, and when the fire was hot
and smokeless huddled in ranks against
the cold at the top of the chimney. And they're not
without gratitude. Though I'm clearly visible

to them now, they swirl on and sing,
and if, in the early dusk, I should fall
on my way back home and—injured, weeping—
rail against the stars and the frigid night
and crawl a while on my hopeless way
then stop, numb, easing into the darkening white
like a candle, I know they'll stay
with me, keeping watch, moving limb to limb,
angels down Jacob's ladder, wise
to the moon, and waiting for me, simple as sin,
that they may know the delicacy of my eyes.

Marie Winn

FROM *RED-TAILS IN LOVE* (1998)

THE NAME of the game in birdwatching is telling one species of bird from another. This one's a chickadee; that one's a nuthatch. But only by marking birds in some way, usually by attaching bands to their legs, can individual birds within a species be distinguished from each other. Generally one robin looks like any other, or one downy woodpecker, or one red-tailed hawk.

Every so often it happens that a particular bird displays some feature that makes it recognizable as an individual. Sometimes there's an injury—a duck with a broken wing; sometimes a genetic anomaly—an albino sparrow; sometimes it's simply a natural oddity of size or shape or color. People may follow the course of such birds' lives in a way that would be impossible if they looked just like their species-mates.

Such a one was the red-tailed hawk that arrived in Central Park during my first winter as a Regular. He had a feature so distinctive he could always be identified—not just as a red-tailed hawk but as himself, a particular, individual bird. Whereas this species appears in field guides with a white breast, a broad band of streaks across the belly, and a darkish head, this particular red-tail was exceptionally light all over. His head was almost white. He had no belly-band to speak of—the breast and belly were white. He wasn't an albino, his eyes were too brown; just a very pale red-tail.

Tom Fiore saw him first, and reported his sighting in the Bird Register on November 10th:

There is a very light-colored, immature red-tailed hawk
that has been seen eating a rat and also swooping a foot
above shoveler ducks on the lake.

How did Tom know the light-colored hawk was immature? Was
it smaller?

It's a common misconception that all young birds are smaller
than adults of their species. Though it is true for ducks, geese, and
birds that leave the nest shortly after hatching, most songbirds and
birds of prey, indeed, the majority of the avian order, cannot leave
the nest until their flight feathers grow in. These birds are full adult
size by the time they take their first flight.

It is the plumage of most immature birds, not their size, that
clearly distinguishes them from the adults. Young birds generally
lack whatever bright colors adults of their species might display,
making them less conspicuous during the vulnerable nestling and
fledgling periods. Young robins have speckles on their breast rather
than the characteristic solid brick red coloring of adult robins; juve-
nile male cardinals are buffy brown, not bright red, as their fathers
are. Immature red-tailed hawks contradict their name: their tails
are brown, and won't turn red until they are two years old—breed-
ing age. Moreover, the tails of immature red-tails are marked with
distinct black bands. One look at the pale-colored red-tail's tail
revealed to Tom that this one was a kid.

For a while Tom was not sure whether the young hawk he'd
sighted on November 10th was a male or a female. Among most
birds of prey, males and females do not significantly differ in plumage or markings. Still, there *is* a way to tell the sexes apart: Female
raptors are almost always bigger than males. Consequently, when a
second and noticeably larger hawk arrived in the park a few months
later, the sex of the pale-colored bird became perfectly clear. The
Regulars began to call him Pale Male.

He was still a browntail that spring, too young for love. Nevertheless and notwithstanding, when the female (this one with a bright red tail) showed up at the beginning of March, Pale Male courted and won her.

The first junco trill was noted by Norma Collin on March 9th that year, right on schedule. One week and one day later Pale Male and his new mate made their decision. They'd been checking the place out for a few months now and things looked good. Plenty of food around—corn-fed pigeons and garbage-fed rats. A lake to bathe in. Protection available from wind and storms. Time to get the show on the road. On March 17th the hawk pair began to build a nest in Central Park. It was a historic event, for in the 119 years of the park's existence, no hawk had ever nested there before.

They made an odd couple, a mature female who had hooked up with a young and inexperienced male. His lack of savoir-faire was evident: on March 23rd, as the female was perched on a stanchion in front of the Delacorte Theater below Belvedere Castle, the light-colored red-tail was observed as he landed on top of her and tried to consummate their union. But he was doing it at the wrong end.

Perhaps lack of experience also explains the absurdly conspicuous spot the birds chose for that historic first home in Central Park: a tree just behind the baseball backstop at the southwest corner of the Great Lawn.

A grassy expanse filled, on nice afternoons and weekends, with kids playing Frisbee, muscular men in shorts and knee socks playing soccer, and various groups enjoying pickup games of baseball, the Great Lawn is hardly an auspicious nest site for a bird long thought to be highly sensitive to the human presence. "It is one of the shyest of our hawks," wrote Arthur Cleveland Bent in *Life Histories of North American Birds of Prey.* "If [red-tails] suspect that the nest is watched they will not come near it." That was in 1937. The species had obviously adapted to new circumstances over the years, for these Central Park red-tails were oblivious to the hundreds of humans in the vicinity. Most of those humans were equally unaware of them.

The park's birdwatchers, however, took notice. They watched the hawks bringing sticks to the nest. They timed the increasingly successful though invariably brief love acts. They saw them hunting for pigeons and making occasional dives at local squirrels. Accustomed to receiving handouts in perfect safety, the Central Park squirrel corps was totally unprepared for becoming handouts themselves for resident birds of prey. And as the first migratory birds of spring, the woodcock and the eastern phoebe, began to trickle into the park, the Regulars saw that these much-awaited visitors had something new to contend with. As Tom Fiore noted in the Register on March 25th:

> While bluejays in nearby trees were screaming . . . the pale [immature] Red-tail came flying up from those trees and landed on a mat of broken phragmites in Belvedere Pond. . . . I sat down at the edge of the rocks below the Castle and a Woodcock flew from behind me right over the young hawk, toward the north shore of the pond . . . the young hawk flew right up and chased after the woodcock, pursuing it through some trees on the south shore. . . . an Eastern Phoebe was catching something too small to see, moving around the area below the Castle. Then the young Red-tail went after *it*, but the Phoebe merely landed on a little outcrop of rock below the Castle and the hawk was forced to veer off.

On April 2nd Norma Collin's Register entry made it clear that Pale Male had acquired some new skills:

> Red-tailed hawks *mating* on Delacorte tower. Mature
> female (with red tail) stayed near nest. Male circled and
> returned and they mated again!! So keep watching!

But by April 4th it was obvious that the Great Lawn nest was a
bust. The flimsy structure was falling apart. That was the day Sylvia and Mo Cohen, birdwatchers who go back to the old Lambert
Pohner days, found a broken egg at the base of the backstop. They
brought it to the next meeting of the Linnaean Society, where one
of the club's officers examined the fragment and said: "This proves
that anything's possible in Central Park."

Less than a week later, a Register entry revealed that the indom-
itable pair had not given up.

> There's another *nest* being built by Red-tailed hawks in the
> park. I'm not saying where it is for now. Perhaps you've
> already discovered it?   Tom Fiore

Tom was clearly worried that birdwatcher attention may have con-
tributed to the failure at the Great Lawn. Perhaps secrecy would
help, at least in the early stages of nest building, he decided. But two
days later someone else described the new nest site in the Register:

> Red-tail in nest! East drive, slightly north of marker 6902—
> west side of Drive—(elm).   Murray and Dave

On April 14th Tom relented and wrote in a detailed description
of the new nest site:

> Red-tailed Hawk on *nest*—high in (Elm?) tree—large, dark
> bark with deep furrows. It's between 2 large London Plane
> trees just 15 feet or so west of the East Drive (opposite E.

70th Street). There are daffodils planted nearby and a new water fountain on the path just west of the nest tree.

The next day Tom drew a map of the nest location in the Register, though he still worried about the consequences of too much human attention. "Please don't make a lot of noise if the hawks are seen," he wrote in large letters beside the map. It seemed an unnecessary injunction since the birds' new location was directly adjacent to SummerStage, a park facility where noisy crowds often gather and ear-shattering rock concerts are held on summer weekends.

A group of Regulars began gathering daily to watch the birds at the nest. By the end of the second week of April the large structure of sticks and twigs near the crown of the tree seemed complete. This time, the nest looked more solid. Everyone made efforts to be quiet in the vicinity, and those who forgot themselves were "shushed" into submission. But had the hawks built a home as strong as Fort Knox and had they enjoyed a human audience as silent as the grave, their efforts would still have been doomed. They were done in by members of their own class: crows.

Crows are natural enemies of hawks, and little mobs of them are often seen in furious pursuit of birds of prey. Yet these crows seemed exceptionally vicious. From the first day the hawk pair tried to settle in at their new nest site, the entire crow nation seemed to have declared total war. There proved to be a reason for the ferocity of the crows' attacks: they had a lien on that territory, for the previous year a pair of crows had nested in the same elm. Now, as the birdwatchers watched the screaming squadrons of crows persecuting the hawks, they lavished pity on the nesting pair, quite forgetting that hawks have a savage side of their own.

The hawks persevered, and by the end of April their behavior made it clear that there were eggs in the nest. One hawk would arrive, the sitting one would take off, whereupon the arriving bird would settle down to keep the eggs warm—nest exchanges, these are called.

The crows persevered as well. At each nest exchange, the crows hounded the departing hawk, their screams ever louder and more insistent. The end came on May 2nd, when the female hawk was so flummoxed by her crow persecutors that she crashed into a wall at the top of a high-rise on Fifth Avenue and 73rd Street.

Witnesses in an adjoining building called the New York City Audubon Society, which in turn called a local wildlife rehabilitator, Vivienne Sokol. But when she arrived it was clear that the injured hawk was beyond first aid. Something was seriously wrong with the bird's left wing, which hung at a weird angle to the side. Miss Sokol packed the bird into a large cardboard carton and took her away.

A few days later a particularly vociferous gang of crows, perhaps emboldened by their successful rout of the female hawk, pursued Pale Male until he too crashed into a building, this one at 62nd Street near Madison Avenue.

A woman I ran into by chance a few years later told me the whole story. She then worked for an ear-nose-throat doctor in that building, a Dr. Blaugrund. At around noon on May 4th she heard crows screaming bloody murder just outside the waiting room. She ran to the window and instead of crows she saw a large brownish bird lying on the rooftop of a town house below. She too called the Audubon Society, and then all work stopped at the doctor's office as everyone—doctor, nurses, and patients—stood by the window, watching the unconscious hawk. Things did not return to normal until the wildlife rehabilitator arrived, the same one, it turned out, who had taken charge of the injured female.

Pale Male had merely suffered a concussion. Miss Sokol applied first aid and gave him a few days to recover at her home. The female hawk was beyond local help. The rehabilitator packed the bird back in a large carton and drove her to the Raptor Trust, a well-known hawk hospital in Millington, New Jersey. If anyone could help the bird it would be Len Soucy, the founder and director of the facility.

The Regulars were stunned at the sudden conclusion of the red-tail affair. It had been a thrilling story. But everyone knew that other stories were happening elsewhere in the park. They just had to keep their eyes and ears open. And at least Pale Male was back in the park. "Hallelujah," said Charles Kennedy, a man given to exultation and to looking on the bright side of dismal events.

Richard Wilbur

A BARRED OWL (2000)

The warping night air having brought the boom
Of an owl's voice into her darkened room,
We tell the wakened child that all she heard
Was an odd question from a forest bird,
Asking of us, if rightly listened to,
"Who cooks for you?" and then "Who cooks for you?"

Words, which can make our terrors bravely clear,
Can also thus domesticate a fear,
And send a small child back to sleep at night
Not listening for the sound of stealthy flight
Or dreaming of some small thing in a claw
Borne up to some dark branch and eaten raw.

Louise Erdrich

I WAS SLEEPING WHERE THE BLACK OAKS MOVE (2003)

We watched from the house
as the river grew, helpless
and terrible in its unfamiliar body.
Wrestling everything into it,
the water wrapped around trees
until their life-hold was broken.
They went down, one by one,
and the river dragged off their covering.

Nests of the herons, roots washed to bones,
snags of soaked bark on the shoreline:
a whole forest pulled through the teeth
of the spillway. Trees surfacing
singly, where the river poured off
into arteries for fields below the reservation.

When at last it was over, the long removal,
they had all become the same dry wood.
We walked among them, the branches
whitening in the raw sun.
Above us drifted herons,
alone, hoarse-voiced, broken,
settling their beaks among the hollows.

Grandpa said, *These are the ghosts of the tree people*
moving among us, unable to take their rest.

Sometimes now, we dream our way back to the heron dance.
Their long wings are bending the air
into circles through which they fall.
They rise again in shifting wheels.
How long must we live in the broken figures
their necks make, narrowing the sky.

Debra Nystrom

CLIFF SWALLOWS (2003)

Missouri Breaks

Is it some turn of wind
that funnels them all down at once, or
is it their own voices netting
to bring them in—the roll and churr
of hundreds searing through river light
and cliff dust, each to its precise
mud nest on the face—
none of our isolate
human groping, wishing need could be sent
so unerringly to solace. But
this silk-skein flashing is like heaven
brought down: not to meet ground
or water—to enter
the earth and disappear.

Mark Jarman

A PAIR OF TANAGERS (2004)

The scarlet male, his green mate, their black wings
Beside the AC unit in the dull dirt:

They look at first like a child's abandoned toys.
But ants and iridescent flies have found them,

Working along the seams of the shut beaks
And the dark indentations of the eyelids.

You want to give something like this a moral:
Like, the woods these days are full of hard illusions,

Or, never fly north if you think you're flying south,
Or, stay above rooftops; if you meet yourself

Coming, it's too late; death is a big surprise.
And their death together certainly startles us.

Stopped short. But how recently in the rain forest,
How recently in the place they were first named,

Reflected on the Amazon, the Orinoco,
Headlong from Brazil, into our window.

You want to give something like this a moral
Or see it as an omen, as a portent.

And then, the long journeying comes to mind,
Together such a distance, to this end.

Ted Kooser

SCREECH OWL (2004)

All night each reedy whinny
from a bird no bigger than a heart
flies out of a tall black pine
and, in a breath, is taken away
by the stars. Yet, with small hope
from the center of darkness
it calls out again and again.

Pamela Uschuk

SNOW GOOSE MIGRATION AT TULE LAKE (2005)

Iris-eyed dawn and the slow blind buffalo of fog
shoulders along flat turned fields.
We hear the bassoon a cappella
before air stutters

                     to the quake that wheels.

Then the thermonuclear flash of snow geese,
           huge white confetti,

                  storm and tor of black tipped wings
                    across Shasta's silk peak,
                        the bulging half moon.

There are thousands. Now
        no stutter but ululations
               striking as the riot of white water.
Wave on wave breaks
over us. V

            after V interlock, weave
               like tango dancers to dip and rise
                    as their voices hammer
silver jewelry in our hearts. These multitudes
            drown every sound, stop
                 every twenty-first century complaint.

Snow geese unform us.
Fluid our hands, our arms, legs,
                    our hearts. What more do we ever need?
Than these songs
                    cold and pure as Arctic-bladed warriors
                        circling the lake's mercuric eye.

Snake graceful in the sky, snow geese wail
                    through sunrise like tribal women
                            into funeral flames.
Sun rouges their feathers
            as they rise
                            hosannahward, dragging us
stunned by the alchemy of their clamour.

And we think
how it must have been each season
for eight hundred years while Modocs harvested wild rice
                    blessed by the plenty of wings
                    on the plenty of water
before slaughter moved in with the settlers.
The few Modoc survivors were exiled to Oklahoma
to make way for potato farms
                            that even now poison the soil
and drain Tule Lake.

In this month of wild plum blossoms, we would pretend
it is the early world.
            Snow geese migrate through sky wide
as memory. Their wild choirs lift us
            beyond the dischords of smoking fields and tractors
to light struck white, to our own forgotten wings
and ungovernable shine.

Robert Cording

PEREGRINE FALCON, NEW YORK CITY (2006)

On the 65th floor where he wrote
Advertising copy, joking about
The erotic thrall of words that had
No purpose other than to make
Far too many buy far too much,
He stood one afternoon face to face
With a falcon that veered on the blade
Of its wings and plummeted, then
Swerved to a halt, wings hovering.

An office of computers clicked
Behind him. Below, the silence
Of the miniature lunch time crowds
And toy-like taxis drifting without
Resolve to the will of others.
This bird's been brought in, he thought,
To clean up the city's dirty problems
Of too many pigeons. It's a hired beak.

Still he remained at the tinted glass
Windows, watching as the falcon
Gave with such purpose its self
To the air that carried it, its sheer falls
Breaking the mirrored self-reflections

Of glass office towers. He chided
Himself: this is how the gods come
To deliver a message or a taunt,
And, for a moment, the falcon
Seemed to wait for his response,
The air articulate with a kind of
Wonder and terror. Then it was gone.

He waited at the glass until he felt
The diminishment of whatever
Had unsettled him. And though
The thin edge of the falcon's wings
Had opened the slightest fissure in him
And he'd wandered far in thought,
He already felt himself turning back
To words for an ad, the falcon's power
Surely a fit emblem for something.

Ursula K. Le Guin

THE CACTUS WREN (2006)

(Joshua Tree National Park)

In this great silence, to sit still
and listen till I hear the wren
is to draw free from wish and will.

She flits to perch; her slender bill
spouts a thin jet of music; then
in the great silence she falls still.

Wind nods the short-stemmed flowers that fill
the sandy wash. She sings again
her song devoid of wish or will.

The hummingbird's quick drum and thrill
is gone just as I hear it, when
in this great silence all holds still.

The granite sand, the barren hill,
the dry, vast, rigorous terrain
answer no human wish or will.

Again, the small quicksilver trill
that has no messages for men.
In the great silence she sings still
of pure need free from wish or will.

Timothy Steele

BLACK PHOEBE (2006)

Her swoops are short and low and don't aspire
To more, it seems, than nature's common strife.
Perching, she strops her bill across a wire
As though she'd barbered in a former life.
When the wire rocks, she quickly dips her tail
A few times, and her balance doesn't fail.

If she displays an unassuming pride—
Compact, black-capped, black breast puffed to the sun—
The sentiment perhaps is justified:
Mosquitoes, gnats, and flies would overrun
Much of the planet within several years
But for her and her insectivorous peers.

Not prone, as are the jays, to talking trash,
She offers quieter companionship;
On summer days, when starlings flap and splash
And make the birdbath overspill and drip
Or empty out its basin altogether,
She seeks the shade and waits for cooler weather.

When autumn whips the plum tree to and fro
And rains slick its dark trunk, and pools collect
Among its exposed roots, and Mexico

Tempts most birds of the garden to defect,
It is a cheering check against chagrin
To think this is the place she'll winter in.

She makes, for now, a series of abrupt
Dives, lifts, and turns; from a tomato stake,
She spots a moth and darts to interrupt
Its course and then retrieves her perch to make
A thorough survey, though at no great height,
Of plants confided to her oversight.

Richard Powers

FROM *THE ECHO MAKER* (2006)

CRANES KEEP LANDING as night falls. Ribbons of them roll down, slack against the sky. They float in from all compass points, in kettles of a dozen, dropping with the dusk. Scores of *Grus canadensis* settle on the thawing river. They gather on the island flats, grazing, beating their wings, trumpeting: the advance wave of a mass evacuation. More birds land by the minute, the air red with calls.

A neck stretches long; legs drape behind. Wings curl forward, the length of a man. Spread like fingers, primaries tip the bird into the wind's plane. The blood-red head bows and the wings sweep together, a cloaked priest giving benediction. Tail cups and belly buckles, surprised by the upsurge of ground. Legs kick out, their backward knees flapping like broken landing gear. Another bird plummets and stumbles forward, fighting for a spot in the packed staging ground along those few miles of water still clear and wide enough to pass as safe.

Twilight comes early, as it will for a few more weeks. The sky, ice blue through the encroaching willows and cottonwoods, flares up, a brief rose, before collapsing to indigo. Late February on the Platte, and the night's chill haze hangs over this river, frosting the stubble from last fall that still fills the bordering fields. The nervous birds, tall as children, crowd together wing by wing on this stretch of river, one that they've learned to find by memory.

They converge on the river at winter's end as they have for eons, carpeting the wetlands. In this light, something saurian still clings to them: the oldest flying things on earth, one stutter-step away from pterodactyls. As darkness falls for real, it's a beginner's world again, the same evening as that day sixty million years ago when this migration began.

Half a million birds—four-fifths of all the sandhill cranes on earth—home in on this river. They trace the Central Flyway, an hourglass laid over the continent. They push up from New Mexico, Texas, and Mexico, hundreds of miles each day, with thousands more ahead before they reach their remembered nests. For a few weeks, this stretch of river shelters the miles-long flock. Then, by the start of spring, they'll rise and head away, feeling their way up to Saskatchewan, Alaska, or beyond.

This year's flight has always been. Something in the birds retraces a route laid down centuries before their parents showed it to them. And each crane recalls the route still to come.

Tonight's cranes mill again on the braided water. For another hour, their massed calls carry on the emptying air. The birds flap and fidget, edgy with migration. Some tear up frosty twigs and toss them in the air. Their jitters spill over into combat. At last the sandhills settle down into wary, stilt-legged sleep, most standing in the water, a few farther up in the stubbled fields.

A squeal of brakes, the crunch of metal on asphalt, one broken scream and then another rouse the flock. The truck arcs through the air, corkscrewing into the field. A plume shoots through the birds. They lurch off the ground, wings beating. The panicked carpet lifts, circles, and falls again. Calls that seem to come from creatures twice their size carry miles before fading.

By morning, that sound never happened. Again there is only here, now, the river's braid, a feast of waste grain that will carry these flocks north, beyond the Arctic Circle. As first light breaks, the fossils return to life, testing their legs, tasting the frozen air, leaping free, bills skyward and throats open. And then, as if the night took nothing, forgetting everything but this moment, the dawn sandhills start to dance. Dance as they have since before this river started.

Faster than they gathered, the only witnesses disappear. They crowd together on the river for a few weeks, fattening; then they're gone. On an invisible signal, the carpet unravels into skeins. Birds by the thousands thread away, taking their memory of the Platte with them. Half a million cranes disperse across the continent. They press north, a state or more a day. The heartiest will cover thousands more miles, on top of the thousand that brought them to this river.

Cranes that crowded into dense bird cities now scatter. They fly in families, lifelong mates with their one or two offspring, any that have survived the previous year. They head for the tundra, peat bogs and muskegs, a remembered origin. They follow landmarks—water, mountains, woods—places recovered from previous years, by a crane map, inside a crane's head. Hours before the onset of bad weather, they will stop for the day, predicting storms on no evidence. By May, they find the nesting spots they left the previous year.

Spring spreads across the Arctic to their archaic cries. A pair that roosted at the roadside on the night of the accident, near to the overturned truck, home in on a remote stretch of coastal Alaska on the Kotzebue Sound. A seasonal switch flips in their brains as they near their nest. They turn fiercely territorial. They attack even their baffled yearling, the one they have nursed all this way back, driving it off with beak jabs and beating wings.

The blue-gray pair turn brown, from the iron rusting in these bogs. They coat themselves with mud and leaves, seasonal camouflage. Their nest is a moated heap of plants and feathers, three feet wide. They call to each other, with coiled, booming trombone windpipes. They dance, bowing deeply, kicking the brisk salt air, bowing again, leaping, spinning, cowling their wings, their throats arched backward in some impulse between stress and joy: ritual spring at the northern edge of being.

Suppose birds store, fixed as a photograph, the outlines of what they have seen. This pair is in their fifteenth year. They will have five more. By June, two new eggs, spotted gray ovals, will follow all the pairs already laid on this spot, a spot all those earlier years had stored in memory.

The pair take turns, as they always have, caring for the clutch. The northern days lengthen until, by the time the eggs hatch, light is continuous. Two colts emerge, already walking and ravenous. The parents trade off hunting for the voracious young, feeding them constantly—seeds and insects, small rodents, the trapped spare energy of the Arctic.

In July, the younger colt starves to death, killed by his older brother's appetite. It has happened before, in most years: a life begun with fratricide. Alone, the surviving bird shoots up. In two months, he is fledged. As the long northern days collapse, his short test flights expand. Frost forms on the family's nest these nights; ice crusting the bogs. By autumn, the young bird is ready to replace last year's ousted child on the long trip back to winter grounds.

But first the birds molt, reverting to native gray. Something happens to their late-summer brains, and this isolated family of three recovers a larger motion. They shed the solitary need. They feed with others, roosting together at night. They hear nearby families passing overhead, threading the great funnel of the Tanana Valley. One day they lift up and join a self-forming V. They lose themselves in the moving strand. Strands converge in kettles, kettles merge in sheets. Soon, fifty thousand birds a day mass down the startled valley, their prehistoric blasts brilliant and deafening, a sky-wide braided river of cranes, tributaries that run for days.

There must be symbols in the birds' heads, something that says *again.* They trace one single, continuous, repeating loop of plains, mountains, tundra, mountains, plains, desert, plains. On no clear signal, these flocks ascend a slow spiral, great twisting columns of lifting thermals that, with one glance at its parents, the new bird learns to ride.

Once, long ago, as the cranes massed for their autumn departure, they passed above an Aleut girl standing alone in a meadow. The birds flew down on her, beat their wings together, and lifted the girl upward in a great turning cloud, hiding her, trumpeting to drown out her calls. The girl rose on that twisting shaft of air and disappeared into the southward flock. So cranes still circle and call when they leave each autumn, reliving that capture of the humans' daughter.

Jonathan Rosen

FROM *THE LIFE OF THE SKIES* (2008)

EVERYONE IS a birdwatcher, but there are two kinds of bird-watchers: those who know what they are and those who haven't yet realized it. In the United States, a lot of people have realized it—47.8 million Americans, according to the Fish and Wildlife Service—and yet my passion is constantly greeted with surprise. *You?* Perhaps it is because I live in a city and lead an urban life. But why should people wonder that I watch birds? It's like being surprised that someone has sex or goes to the bathroom. The surprise reveals ignorance not so much about birds—their beauty, their abundance, their wild allure—as about human nature. We need, as the great biologist Edward O. Wilson has argued, to affiliate with nature in order to be happy. He calls this phenomenon "biophilia."

The urge to watch birds is all but instinctive, dating, no doubt, from a time when knowing the natural world—what could be eaten and what could eat us, what would heal us and what would bring death—was essential. It is fed by our urge to know, as strong as our urge to eat. Could you imagine a lion stalking prey not out of hunger but out of curiosity? We name things, we classify them. In the Bible Adam gives names to the natural world, imposing a human order on a chaos of life, a kind of second creation.

Birdwatching is as human an activity as there can be. We have one foot in the animal kingdom—where, biologically, we belong—but one foot in a kingdom of our own devising. As Walt Whitman said of himself, we are "both in and out of the game / and watching and wondering at it."

As it turns out, living in a city and watching birds is hardly a contradiction. Modern birdwatching is virtually an urban invention. Institutions of higher learning where bird skins were available, not to mention collection curators who brought their indoor learning outdoors, were virtual prerequisites as birdwatching came of age.

To be bored with London is to be bored with life, said Dr. Johnson. I live in New York City, a metropolis greater than Johnson's London, and I feel the same way about my city—but I feel this way partly because it was in New York City that I discovered birds. More and more I realize that to be bored with birds is to be bored with life. I say birds rather than some generic "nature," because birds are what remain to us. Yes, deer and coyotes show up in the suburbs, you can see grizzlies in Yellowstone Park, and certainly there are bugs galore. But in Central Park, two blocks from my apartment, hundreds of species of birds pass through by the thousands every spring and fall, following ancient migratory routes as old as the Ice Age.

If herds of buffalo or caribou moved seasonally through the park, I'd no doubt go out to see them. But the only remaining wild animals in abundance that carry on in spite of human development are birds. The rain forest is far away, but these birds, who often winter there, bring it with them. Here is the nature my biophiliac soul needs to affiliate with. In our mother's womb we float in water, a remnant of our aquatic origins that we somehow took with us when we left the oceans that spawned us eons ago. But where are the woods, the fertile forests that also constituted the womb of our species? Birds bring us fragments, not in their beaks, but on their backs. Tiny fragments, to be sure, and not enough to reconstitute a world—but something.

Emerson said that if the stars appeared in the night sky only once every thousand years, we would "preserve for many generations the remembrance of the city of God." But the stars come out every night, and as it is, many of us scarcely look up; if we do, we find a sky so crowded with artificial light that we hardly notice what else is up there.

The stars suddenly came out for me twelve years ago. I was at lunch in Manhattan in late March when I overheard a man say, with great excitement, "The warblers will be coming through Central Park soon." Somehow, for reasons I still can't explain, I knew right then and there that even though I wasn't sure what warblers were, I was going to go and find them.

With uncharacteristic follow-through I signed up for an introduction to birdwatching at the local branch of the Audubon Society in the West Twenties in Manhattan (who even knew such a place existed in New York City?). There were two classes and two field trips. In the classes we were shown slides of birds and then asked, after the image vanished, to draw what we had been shown. I was appalled to discover how bad I was at remembering—that a wood duck has a helmet of feathers almost like a Greek warrior; that a cedar waxwing has a band of yellow at the base of its tail, and a tiny splotch of red on its wing, like sealing wax, from which it gets its name. Even the obvious cardinal—a bird I'd seen my whole life— surprised me; I had never noticed it has not merely a red body but a red bill, and that its face is masked in black.

"Try to be one of the people," said Henry James, "on whom nothing is lost." As a writer I considered myself observant, but how much was lost on me! Birds may be everywhere, but they also—lucky for them—inhabit an alternate universe, invisible to most of us until we learn to look in a new way. And even after I had been shown them, aspects kept eluding me.

It wasn't my eyes, of course, but some larger quality of vision, a capacity for noticing that was like an unused muscle. As a boy I'd loved Sherlock Holmes stories, and my favorite moment was always when Holmes dazzles Watson by telling him that the murderer must have been a tall man with a limp and unclipped fingernails who smoked a cigar (brand always specified). Of course, Sherlock Holmes also explains to his disbelieving friend that he makes a point of not knowing many things—for example, that the earth revolves around the sun. According to Holmes, the attic of the mind can't be too cluttered with extraneous information and ideas if you are going to fill it with important things like details.

Sitting in the classroom I already felt the furniture in my head getting rearranged, a great emptying out and a great filling up—of names and pictures. Is there anything more pleasant than looking? Birdwatching is sanctioned voyeurism. Heading for the subway afterward, I wasn't entirely surprised to see one of the men in the class dart into a topless bar across the street.

Knowledge itself, like looking, has an erotic component. Freud claimed that all curiosity is at root sexual, since the ultimate answer to the ultimate question—where do we come from?—leads us back to our mother's genitals, the sex act that produced us and the womb that harbored us before birth. Birding *is* bound up with the question of origins, leading us back not between our mother's legs but to equally awkward places of beginning, bound up as they are with primordial anxieties about creation and evolution, divinity and mere materialist accident.

Birds are the closest living relatives of the dinosaurs—a shocking fact. Who would have believed that those little feathered beauties have so much in common with the hulking skeletons in the American Museum of Natural History that so enthralled me when I was a child? Perhaps birding is the adult fulfillment of a childhood fascination. Except that birds aren't extinct (though many species teeter on the brink). They're as close to a velociraptor as I'll come. The more you look at birds, the more you feel remnants of their cold-blooded reptile past; the pitiless round eye and mechanical beak somehow tell you that if you were the size of an ant they'd peck you up in a second. And who are *our* nearest relatives? Chimpanzees, with whom we share more than 95 percent of our genetic material. Why else do we feel so drawn to the woods?

None of these thoughts was in my head as I began birding. On the two birding field trips that came with my introduction to birding class—one to Central Park, the other to Jamaica Bay Wildlife Refuge in Queens—it was simply the pleasure of looking that hooked me, even as I discovered that the birds that had seemed so exotic in class were frequently referred to in the guidebook as "common."

At Jamaica Bay—accessible from my apartment by subway—I saw ibises and egrets and snow geese flying against the Manhattan skyline as airplanes from nearby John F. Kennedy Airport took off and landed. I loved that I could see birds against the silhouette of the World Trade Center, incorrectly perceiving this as a poetic juxtaposition of the permanent towers and the evanescent birds. Discovering that you yourself, and the civilization from which you peer out, are as fragile as the birds you are watching is also part of the story—though this was something else I did not realize at the time.

Gradually the strange contradictory elements of birding seeped into me and deepened its rich appeal. Birdwatching, like all great human activities, is full of paradox. You need to be out in nature to do it, but you are dependent on technology—binoculars—and also on the guidebook in your back pocket, which tells you what you're seeing. The challenge of birding has to do with keeping the bird and the book in balance. The book you bring with you draws the birds you see into the library world—a system of names dating from the eighteenth century, when scientists ordered the plant and animal world and labeled them so that anyone in any country would know he was referring to the same bird. But at the same time that you are casting your scientific net over the wild world, the birds are luring you deeper into the woods or the meadow or the swamp. The library world and the wild, nonverbal world meet in the middle when you are birdwatching. We need both sides of this experience to feel whole, being half wild ourselves. Birdwatching is all about the balance.

I should be outside right now. It's a crisp, brilliant day in mid-September and fall migration is in full swing. Central Park, one of the great places in North America to watch birds, is two blocks from my house. Yet here I am, hunched over my computer.

My father, who was a professor of German literature, was very fond of Kafka's parable about Poseidon, the king of the sea, who has never actually *seen* the ocean because he is so busy with the paperwork required for administering it. He eagerly awaits the end of the world so he can go out and have a look. What was true for Poseidon and the sea is true for us and the air, or the earth. In his own life, Kafka—whose name, he was amused to note, was the Czech word for "jackdaw," a crowlike bird of ill omen—dreamed of being a "red Indian" galloping across the American plain. Instead, he spent his brief tubercular life working in an insurance office in Prague or chained to his writing desk. This is a writer's dilemma—you're drawn to experience but need to be stationary to make sense of it. But writing, like birdwatching, has universal human application. Most people live in cities or suburbs but pine, at some deep level, for the wild world that produced us long ago and that our ancestors, with animal fury, worked so hard to subdue. This is why birding, though it can seem like a token activity, an eccentric pastime, is so central to modern life.

There's a phrase I learned from birding—"binocular vision"—that sounds like it should describe the act of birdwatching itself, but that actually means the ability to see the same thing through both eyes at the same time. Because each image will be slightly different, it gives the looker the capacity for depth perception. If you don't have binocular vision, things need to be in motion for you to notice them, and catch them. The *Tyrannosaurus rex* in *Jurassic Park* (though not necessarily in life) lacked binocular vision, and so if you stayed very still—like the children in *Jurassic Park*—you could avoid detection. The velociraptors had binocular vision, so if you didn't hide, you'd get eaten.

Most birds have some binocular vision—we may have evolved ours leaping from tree to tree and catching food up in the branches, and birds needed their eyes even more—but birds, especially vulnerable ones, have other needs, like seeing what's swooping down or sneaking up on them, and so they sacrifice a large area of overlapping vision for astonishing peripheral vision. The eyes of woodcocks are spaced so far apart, they see behind them better than in front and can look up with their bills stuck in the mud. A pigeon can see 300 degrees, but needs to bob its head to get a sense of depth. Predators tend to have better binocular vision than prey; owls have eyes on the same plane, like us, which makes them master hunters.

We, needless to say, have binocular vision even without binoculars, but I often think of the phrase in a metaphorical way, to mean the sort of double vision that birding requires. One of the best descriptions of this double vision was provided by the writer Harold Brodkey in his memoir about dying of AIDS:

> At one time I was interested in bird-watching, and I noticed that when I saw a bird for the first time I couldn't really see it, because I had no formal arrangement, no sense of pattern, for it. I couldn't remember it clearly, either. But once I identified the bird, the drawings in bird books and my own sense of order arranged the image and made it clearer to me, and I never forgot it. From then on I could

see the bird in two ways—as the fresh, unpatterned vision and the patterned one. Well, seeing death nearby is very like the first way of seeing.

I love this passage because it captures the weird conundrum of birding—that until we know what a bird is, it's hard to recognize it properly when we see it for the first time, but until we've seen it for the first time, it's hard to know what it is. For Brodkey, death, that ultimate undiscovered country, could never be seen properly because he'd never been there before. And yet, in his book, he does see it, and lets us see it, too. We are looking for life when we bird, but that very formulation implies the presence of death.

Emily Wilson

RED-LEGGED KITTIWAKE (2009)

1

Native it seems to no part
of the North American continent
but some islets off
the rugged scarps of the Aleutians
in the loose entablatured cliffs
among dwarf-willow tips.
Known if at all by its silhouette
(we can know such things by their silhouettes)
the red-legged kittiwake
glimpsed in isolate parts of Oregon
California and southern Nevada
said to go silent in winter
slitting through snow
the red-legged kittiwake.

2

The red of the red-legged kittiwake
of a kinship with black
solders across the ice-gaps.
Native in no real part
but its obdurate course the red-
legged kittiwake goes silent.
We can know still more by rips

through the weed.
Red-legged kittiwake
gone back in the brain toward
noise of the narrowing ship-lanes.

3
Silver bones of the wrist
in their riggings rotate.
Pulp of the madder-root
shocked in white alum then soaked
through the wool for the waistcoat.
The frigate sprays back gray rime
cuts through the ice-skirt
pursuing such things
to the knit of the nest.

4
Crowberry swollen with fog
lichen resist on the lowest
spokes of the spruce
red-legged kittiwake
native to no part
alone in its parts

5
Kelp closes up
where the bird has just been

6
The legs retract in the pan
of the tail near the crotch
against the streaked ruff

bits of the barbs in breakage
out in the vanes
tipped into place
leaf of the willow tipped into
its branch the tip but tip to its whole

7

So where does it go when gone.
The wake of the factory ships.
Its chevrons compound the steep bluffs
it makes itself into those ranks
like pistons or books.
Its numbers are known to be in decline.
Is red for the advent
of sex or something more plain.

8

The sea works its surface.
Notched and convex.
It gives up its force in forms it must make.
It has a grease shine.
It is where they go when gone isn't it
through the known parts

C. K. Williams

BLACKBIRD (2010)

There was nothing I could have done—
a flurry of blackbirds burst
from the weeds at the edge of a field
and one veered out into my wheel
and went under. I had a moment
to hope he'd emerge as sometimes
they will from beneath the back
of the car and fly off,
but I saw him behind on the roadbed,
the shadowless sail of a wing
lifted vainly from the clumsy
bundle of matter he'd become.

There was nothing I could have done,
though perhaps I was distracted:
I'd been listening to news of the war,
hearing that what we'd suspected
were lies had proved to be lies,
that many were dying for those lies,
but as usual now, it wouldn't matter.
I'd been thinking of Lincoln's
". . . You can't fool all of the people
all of the time . . . ," how I once

took comfort from the hope and trust
it implied, but no longer.

I had to slow down now,
a tractor hauling a load of hay
was approaching on the narrow lane.
The farmer and I gave way and waved:
the high-piled bales swayed
menacingly over my head but held.
Out in the harvested fields,
already disked and raw,
more blackbirds, uncountable
clouds of them, rose, held
for an instant, then broke,
scattered as though by a gale.

Jack Collom

RUDDY DUCK (2012)

or dumpling duck, daub duck, deaf duck,
fool duck, sleepy duck,
butter duck, brown diving teal, widgeon coot,
creek coot, sleepy coot, booby coot,
ruddy diver, dun diver, sleepy brother,
butter-ball, batter-scoot, blatherskite, bumblebee coot,
quail-tailed coot, heavy-tailed coot, stiff-tail,
pin-tail, bristle-tail, sprig-tail, stick-tail, spine-tail, dip-tail,
diver, dun-bird, dumb-bird, mud-dipper,
spoon-billed butter-ball, spoonbill, broad-billed dipper,
dipper, dapper, dopper, broad-bill, blue-bill,
sleepy-head, tough-head, hickory-head,
steel-head, hard-headed broad-bill, bull-neck,
leather-back, paddy-whack, stub-and-twist,
lightwood-knot, shot-pouch, water-partridge,
dinky, dickey, paddy, noddy, booby, rook, roody,
stiff-tailed widgeon, gray teal, salt-water-teal

nest: in the abandoned homes of coots

gunners near the mouth of the Maumee River
found them floundering helplessly fat
on the water

feeds upon delicate grasses

Rick Bass

ANSWERING THE CALL (2013)

THE BIRDERS ARE OLD, intensely alert. Twenty or more of them move through the brush slowly, weaving like dreams. They have arisen early to meet their passion. It's cold—a February dawn, down near the Arizona-Mexico border, south of Tucson. Whenever there is movement back in the brush, the birders all stop and watch, waiting—some keen-eyed with binoculars still hanging from their necks, others with binocs already raised, their eyes gifted suddenly with the quick-sightedness of gods—and no matter how drab or dull the first bird of the day may seem to me, a non-birder, to the old people, these veterans of beauty, it seems amazing. They rhapsodize about sparrows.

They've been coming here for a long time, down near Madera Canyon, one of the premier birding spots in the world: well over 400 species funnel through here, twice a year. A local industry worth $3 billion a year: gazing at passing-through beauty that possesses a fiery heart, a will to survive. It is here that the proposed Rosemont copper mine will suck up the water supply to bathe the damaged soil and stone in acid, yielding the glitter we affix to our wrists and fingers and necks in order to feel beautiful.

Some of the old people are couples who hold hands as they walk along the birding trail. Others are friends, each of whom rests a steadying hand on another's shoulder. They stand peering into the brush as if into the great mystery of their lives, hoping that in time an answer will present itself. My informal survey indicates that most of them believe the Rosemont mine cannot be stopped. Every one of them will do what they can do, but they have been defending beauty and integrity for a long time, and they have seen a lot of loss.

I will likely never see any of these old people again.

Sometimes I get tired of arguing for or against things, and yet it seems I always answer the call, always show up whenever there's a fight, or a need to stand and defend. Might I one day feel tired and worn out, my imagination dimming so that I might not be able to envision a way to win?

The beauty of the birds at Madera Canyon feels to me like a little oasis or wellspring where we stop and sit before pushing on in our own migrations. Ruby-crowned Kinglet. Say's Phoebe. Some kind of pipit. Vesper Sparrow, Lincoln's Sparrow, House Finch, female cardinal: one by one, the birds are stirring, going about their business, taking little dust baths, feeding, singing, courting. There's a dew and in the rising sun the grass blades ignite, rainbow prisms incandesce, and the birds fly up as if uninterested in these temporary jewels that will dull quickly as the sun rises higher.

We peer through sunflowers as if into a kaleidoscope. Ladder-backed Woodpecker, Gila Woodpecker, Savannah Sparrow, kestrel. We cross over a narrow wooden footbridge where there used to be deep water, but where now there is only a web of cracked mud-plates. A man named Al tells me he used to see mallards, snipe, rail here. Today there is nothing, just dust. We move on, searching, or rather, looking.

An owl—no one's sure what kind—leaps up from the grass and flies away into the sun. No one, not even here among the experts, is willing to make a guess, and they squint after it eagerly, hoping for a second clue, hoping it might for some strange reason turn around and come back, but it does not.

Just to the south, a great anti-immigration wall has been constructed, physically dividing one county from another. It blocks the flow of humans back and forth, and impedes the natural passage of animals that for hundreds of thousands of years have passed across that invisible line with the freedom of birds: jaguar, ocelot, coatimundi, Sonoran antelope, wolf, bear. Now all are cut off, all isolated. Only the birds can pass over and through, and where they are coming, there is already often no water. They come following the old pathways of memory, or perhaps hope.

The old birders tell me that often on these outings they encounter people who have crossed the border illegally following these brushy water courses, or courses where water once ran. Immigrant trails exist everywhere here. Lawrence's Goldfinches, Lesser Goldfinches, the birds far more brilliant than the mineral for which they are named, flash and rise and fall, sparks among the brush, delighting the brief humming life of our brains.

Great Horned Owl. Bewick's Wren singing with a song like an old-time rotary dial telephone. How much change these old people have seen, how much more we will all see. Of course everything is temporal, everything is flux, but surely too at some point to stand quietly in the face of violence and injustice is to condone it with that silence.

We come to a barbed-wire fence and note where the prongs have snagged not only the hair of deer but also scraps of faded shirts: a natural history of exodus.

Black Phoebe, Cooper's Hawk. White-crowned Sparrow, Green-tailed Towhee. Later in the spring, Flame-colored Tanager, Elegant Trogon, 36 species of wood warblers, and an entire planet's worth of hummingbirds.

In war, one has to write or speak about war, but one has to write or speak about beauty, too. When to do which? No one knows, I think. Perhaps you know only each morning upon awakening. We must have courage, we must have fire, we must have energy. There is a war and all hearts are tempted to grow numb, to withdraw and tuck in as if about to roost for the long night. We must not allow this to happen. We must burn, we must travel on, with morning's fire in our hearts and beauty everywhere we turn, amidst a great burning.

Wendell Berry

THE ACADIAN FLYCATCHER, NOT (2013)

The Acadian flycatcher, not
a spectacular bird, not a great
singer, is seen only when
alertly watched for. His call
is hardly a song—
a two-syllable squeak you hear
only when listened for.
His back is the color of a leaf
in shadow, his belly that
of a leaf in light. He is here
when the leaves are here, belonging
as the leaves belong, is gone when
they go. His is the voice
of this deep place among
the tiers of summer foliage
where three streams come together.
You sit and listen to the voice
of the water, and then you hear
the voice of the bird. He is saying
to his mate, to himself, to any who
may want to know: "I'm here!"

David Tomas Martinez

OF MOCKINGBIRDS (2014)

By my roofs and poles

a few murders
of crows occurred.

With the forensics of feet
pigeons investigate

the scene, chalking
an outline of feathers,

analyzing splatter
patterns of trash.

The wind moans longingly;

there is no evidence
of tomorrow.

Burgles of cats
scratch a furniture
of cloud and night air;

dogs, loose from packs,
butts put out on the ground,
roll over in the gutters,

and a mockingbird,
darkening a drag of wires,

croons a tune from his
pompadour and beak.

A freestyle from the beat
of leaves and trees,

away from the origins
of the bird's own tongue,

he beeps, whistles, and chimes.
In this mickey fickey of sagged

pants and homemade tattoos,
the haggard muse
tickles his beautiful black ear

with a car's alarm.

Sidney Wade

INDIGO BUNTING (2017)

blue as paint
blue as flame

blue as blue dawn
blue as the burn

after lightning
blue on fire

blue and a black beak
blue on electric wire

blue as the sky
just after dark

blue on the back
of the eye

blue as sleep
blue as a skyblue

dancer no bluer
blue as a sunning shark

blue as Nolde's
watercolor

blue shot
blue bead

bluer than the deep
indigo sea

blue as speed
blue fizz

blue black blue
dart and sizzle

Noah Strycker

FROM *BIRDING WITHOUT BORDERS* (2017)

I SHOULD HAVE KNOWN that my worst flight nightmare would come true in the United States. After months of smooth sailing with any number of dubious-looking airlines in Latin America, the wheels finally came off in New York. There, courtesy of United Airlines, I experienced the real-life embodiment of the nine circles of travel hell.

I couldn't seem to get out of the state. My first flight from Ithaca was delayed, then canceled, because the crew failed to show up. Rather than rebook me onto a flight with a later departure, the ticket agent stuffed me into a taxi bound for a completely different airport, where I waited out the rest of the afternoon, only to learn that a second flight was delayed, then canceled, because of thunderstorms. After that, in exasperation, I caught a Greyhound bus to New York City, arrived in the pelting rain at 2 A.M., crashed for a couple of hours at a Manhattan hotel, and managed to fly out the next day. By then I had been delayed for twenty-seven hours. It was a short, infinitely short, period of time in the space of a whole life, but an excruciating epoch within the confines of the Big Year.

None of this seemed to bother United in the least. Didn't they realize that time was of the essence? I had become a slave to time, and my blood was boiling. The airline that boasts the most flights to the most destinations around the world had offered me no flights to any destination, and in so doing had landed me with my second zero day of the year. Wasting time in airports wasn't quite what I'd envisioned for my last stop in the Western Hemisphere.

At least the previous day had gone well. After leaving home in Oregon, not to return until this year was over, I'd landed in Ithaca to meet Tim Lenz, a full-time programmer for the Cornell Lab of Ornithology's website, eBird, which I was using to track my sightings for the year. Tim spends his free time birding his brains out and knew where to find the species I sought in New York, partly because he'd catalogued them all in eBird. He was wiry, precise, and about the same age as me.

The two of us were near Cayuga Lake, looking for common birds such as Upland Sandpipers and American Black Ducks, when Tim received a WhatsApp message on his phone.

"Wow," he said, suddenly at full attention. "It looks like someone just reported a Brown Pelican flying over the lake. That's, like, the first inland record for New York! We've got to go see that bird!"

"Nice!" I said, and then I paused. "But, Tim, I just saw thousands of Brown Pelicans on the Pacific Ocean last week, where they're supposed to be. I don't need one for the year list. I do need to see American Black Ducks today because it's my last chance . . ."

Tim looked stricken. In this situation, it wasn't immediately clear which should take priority: a mega-rare species in New York for his life list or an ultra-common addition for my Big Year list.

"But it's a Brown Pelican!" he protested. "Do you realize how unusual that is? This might never happen again!"

I sympathized. In Oregon, whenever a rarity is reported, I leap to see it without a second thought. That's the nature of birding. You have to go for it because you don't know if it'll ever happen again. Still, for me, for the Big Year, this pelican sighting was a distraction.

"Maybe we can do both?" I suggested. "Do we have time to race over for the pelican, then go find some black ducks?"

"Yes!" Tim said. "Let's go for it!"

He pulled a big U-turn on the highway and, in moments, we were speeding toward Cayuga Lake on our new mission.

As we drove, Tim's phone blew up with WhatsApp messages from other birders on the pelican trail. Because Ithaca hosts Cornell University, with its famous Lab of Ornithology, the city is packed with birders—and all of them were now looking for the same Brown Pelican. Sightings were reported in real time via instant messages. Someone saw it flying south along the lake; someone else reported it a few miles away. The bird, for its part, apparently was roaming aimlessly around the forty-mile-long lake, probably wondering where it had taken a wrong turn from the ocean, unaware that its cover was blown.

A message pinged from Marshall Iliff and Tom Schulenberg, two of Cornell's elite birders, who suggested we head for a yacht club along the lakeshore. They were stationed up the lake and had just watched the pelican fly over their heads.

"It should pass by there in a couple of minutes if it continues straight," they said.

Tim got us to the marina in a hurry, and we ran onto the docks, scanning the skies. No pelican. How fast can a Brown Pelican fly? We stood there, trying to make hypothetical calculations of speed and distance, when Tim saw a speck on the horizon.

The long bill, dumpy body, and prehistoric-looking wings—even in distant silhouette—confirmed that we had our quarry. As the pelican approached, we raised our cameras like anti-aircraft gunners. The bird lumbered directly overhead, bomber style, giving full-frame views.

Tim was ecstatic.

"No way!" he said. "A Brown Pelican on Cayuga Lake!"

In another minute, it had disappeared in the direction of downtown Ithaca, where the WhatsApp reports kept coming. Someone reported it over the farmers' market, then a student on the Cornell University campus ran out of class and managed to see the bird fly over.

"That's quite a tick for the campus list," said Tim, with a connoisseur's appreciation.

We eventually found the American Black Ducks, for my benefit, but I couldn't stop thinking about that pelican and what it represented. On any scale smaller than the world, a Big Year is all about chasing rarities: if, say, you decided to limit your Big Year to New York State, then this Brown Pelican, or any other rarity, would be a must-see. Drawing the boundaries at the state line automatically puts you in reaction mode, with the imperative to tear off in any direction to witness one lost bird at a time. I have nothing against this sort of birding—I do it all the time—but some critics liken such pursuits to ambulance chasing, and at best it is a game of diminishing returns. Once you've seen all the common birds in a given area, it takes a lot more work and expense to find new ones.

The best way to avoid chasing rare birds is to take on the whole planet. You can go where each bird is supposed to be instead of waiting for a lost vagrant to show up on your doorstep. The world is the only scale that doesn't reward rarity hunts. I liked the idea that, by thinking globally and birding locally, I was helping to reinvent the Big Year as a way to appreciate the most common birds in their proper habitats. It seemed almost subversive, akin to a graffiti artist who paints murals instead of spraying his initials everywhere.

W. S. Merwin

UNKNOWN BIRD (2001)

Out of the dry days
through the dusty leaves
far across the valley
those few notes never
heard here before

one fluted phrase
floating over its
wandering secret
all at once wells up
somewhere else

and is gone before it
goes on fallen into
its own echo leaving
a hollow through the air
that is dry as before

where is it from
hardly anyone
seems to have noticed it
so far but who now
would have been listening

it is not native here
that may be the one
thing we are sure of
it came from somewhere
else perhaps alone

so keeps on calling for
no one who is here
hoping to be heard
by another of its own
unlikely origin

trying once more the same few
notes that began the song
of an oriole last heard
years ago in another
existence there

it goes again tell
no one it is here
foreign as we are
who are filling the days
with a sound of our own

Sources and Acknowledgments

I am grateful to the following individuals for help in putting together this anthology: Lucienne Bloch, John Kulka, Bruno Navasky, Eric Ozawa, Will Papp, Marc Passmann, Melissa Peters, Barbara Saunders, and Rick Wright,

And mostly to Michael Psareas—and that second pair of binoculars.
—Andrew Rubenfeld

John James Audubon, from *Mississippi River Journal* (1820–21), ed. Christopher Irmscher (New York: Library of America, 1999). Copyright © 1999 by Literary Classics of the United States, Inc. "Ivory-billed Woodpecker," *Ornithological Biography* (Edinburgh: Adam Black, 1831–39).

Rick Bass, "Answering the Call," *Tricycle*, Fall 2013. Copyright © by Rick Bass. Used by permission of the author.

Wendell Berry, "The Acadian flycatcher, not," *This Day: Collected & New Sabbath Poems* (Berkeley: Counterpoint Press, 2013). Copyright © 2013 by Wendell Berry. Reprinted by permission of Counterpoint Press.

Elizabeth Bishop, "Sandpiper," *Poems* (New York: Farrar, Straus and Giroux, 2011). Copyright © 2011 by The Alice H. Methfessel Trust. Publisher's Note and compilation copyright © 2011 by Farrar, Straus and Giroux. Reprinted by permission of Farrar, Straus and Giroux.

Sterling A. Brown, "Idyll," *The Collected Poems of Sterling A. Brown,* edited by Michael S. Harper (New York: Harper & Row, 1980). Copyright © 1980 by Sterling A. Brown. Reprinted by permission of the Estate of Sterling A. Brown.

William Cullen Bryant, "To a Waterfowl," *Poems* (Cambridge, MA: Hilliard and Metcalf, 1821).

John Burroughs, "Wild Life about My Cabin," *Far and Near* (Boston: Houghton Mifflin Company, 1904).

Rachel Carson, "Flood Tide" (Chapter 1), *Under the Sea Wind: 50th Anniversary Edition* (New York: Dutton, 1991). Copyright © 1941 by Rachel L. Carson. Copyright © renewed 1969 by Roger Christie. Used by permission of Dutton, an imprint of Penguin Publishing Group, a division of Penguin Random House LLC. All rights reserved.

Lorna Dee Cervantes, "Emplumada," *Emplumada* (Pittsburgh: University of Pittsburgh Press, 1981). Copyright © 1981 by Lorna Dee Cervantes. Reprinted by permission of the University of Pittsburgh Press.

Frank M. Chapman, from *Handbook of the Birds of Eastern North America* (New York: D. Appleton and Company, 1895; second edition, 1912; revised edition, 1924).

Amy Clampitt, "Shorebird-Watching," *The Collected Poems of Amy Clampitt* (New York: Alfred A. Knopf, 1997). Copyright © 1997 by the Estate of Amy Clampitt. Used by permission of Alfred A. Knopf, an imprint of the Knopf Doubleday Publishing Group, a division of Penguin Random House LLC. All rights reserved.

Jack Collom, "Ruddy Duck," *Second Nature* (Berkeley: Instance Press, 2012). Copyright © by Jack Collom. Used by permission of Jennifer Heath Collom and The Estate of Jack Collom.

Robert Cording, "Peregrine Falcon, New York City," *Common Life* (Fort Lee, NJ: CavanKerry Press, 2006). Copyright © 2000, 2006 by Robert Cording. Reprinted with the permission of The Permissions Company, Inc., on behalf of CavanKerry Press, Ltd., www.cavankerry.org.

Robert Creeley, "The Birds," *Collected Poems of Robert Creeley, 1945–2005* (Berkeley: University of California Press, 2008). Copyright © 2008 by The Regents of University of California. Republished with permission of University of California Press via the Copyright Clearance Center, Inc.

J. Hector St. John de Crèvecoeur, from *Letters from an American Farmer* (London: Thomas Davies and Lockyer Davis, 1782).

Emily Dickinson, "A Bird came down the Walk-" (written c. 1862) and "The Way to know the Bobolink" (written c. 1873), *The Poems of Emily Dickinson: Variorum Edition*, ed. R. W. Franklin (Cambridge: Harvard University Press, 1998). Copyright © 1998 by the President and Fellows of Harvard College. Copyright © 1951, 1955 by the President and Fellows of Harvard College. Copyright © renewed 1979, 1983 by the President and Fellows of Harvard College. Copyright © 1914, 1918, 1919, 1924, 1929, 1930, 1932, 1935, 1937, 1942 by Martha Dickinson Bianchi. Copyright © 1952, 1957, 1958, 1963, 1965 by Mary L. Hampson. Used by permission.

Cornelius Eady, "Crows in a Strong Wind," *Victims of the Latest Dance Craze* (Chicago: Ommation Press, 1986). Copyright © 1986 by Cornelius Eady. Used by permission of the author.

Ralph Waldo Emerson, from *Selected Journals 1820–1842*, ed. Lawrence Rosenwald (New York: Library of America, 2010). Copyright © 2010 by Literary Classics of the United States, Inc. and *Selected Journals 1841–1877*, ed. Lawrence Rosenwald (New York: Library of America, 2010). Copyright © 2010 by Literary Classics of the United States, Inc. All rights reserved.

Louise Erdrich, "I Was Sleeping Where the Black Oaks Move," *Original Fire* (New York: HarperCollins, 2003). Copyright © 2003 by Louise Erdrich. Reprinted by permission of HarperCollins Publishers.

Robert Frost, "The Oven Bird," *Mountain Interval* (New York: Henry Holt, 1916).

John Haines, "If the Owl Calls Again," *Winter News* (Middletown, CT: Wesleyan University Press, 1966). Copyright © 1966 by John Haines. Published by Wesleyan University Press and reprinted by permission.

Anthony Hecht, "House Sparrows," *Collected Earlier Poems* (New York: Alfred A. Knopf, 1990). Copyright © 1990 by Anthony E. Hecht. Used by permission of Alfred A. Knopf, an imprint of the Knopf Doubleday Publishing Group, a division of Penguin Random House LLC. All rights reserved.

Linda Hogan, "Crow Law," *Book of Medicines* (Minneapolis, MN.: Coffee House Press, 1993). Copyright © 1993 by Linda Hogan. Reprinted with the permission of The Permissions Company, Inc., on behalf of Coffee House Press, www.coffeehousepress.org.

John Hollander, "Swan and Shadow," *Types of Shape* (New York: Atheneum Books, 1968). Copyright © by John Hollander. Published by Yale University Press and reprinted by permission.

Mark Jarman, "A Pair of Tanagers," *Bone Fires: New and Selected Poems* (Louisville: Sarabande Books, 2011). Copyright © 2004 by Mark Jarman. Reprinted with the permission of The Permissions Company, Inc., on behalf of Sarabande Books, Inc., www.sarabandebooks.org.

Randall Jarrell, "The Mockingbird," *The Complete Poems* (New York: Farrar, Straus and Giroux, 1969). Copyright © 1969, renewed 1997 by Mary von S. Jarrell. Reprinted by permission of Farrar, Straus and Giroux.

Robinson Jeffers, "Vulture," *The Beginning and the End* (New York: Random House, 1963). Copyright © 1963 by Garth Jeffers and Donnan Jeffers; from *The Selected Poetry of Robinson Jeffers* by Robinson Jeffers. Used by permission of Random House, an imprint and division of Penguin Random House LLC. All rights reserved.

Sarah Orne Jewett, "A White Heron," *A White Heron and Other Stories* (Boston: Houghton Mifflin Company, 1886).

Ted Kooser, "Screech Owl," *Delights & Shadows* (Port Townsend, WA: Copper Canyon Press, 2004). Copyright © 2004 by Ted Kooser. Reprinted with the permission of The Permissions Company, Inc. on behalf of Copper Canyon Press, www.coppercanyonpress.org.

Sidney Lanier, "The Mocking Bird," *The Poetry of Sidney Lanier*, ed. Mary Day Lanier and W. H. Ward (New York: Charles Scribner's Sons, 1891).

Ursula K. Le Guin, "The Cactus Wren," *Incredible Good Fortune* (Boulder, CO: Shambhala Publications, 2006). Copyright © 2006 by Ursula K. Le Guin. First appeared in *Incredible Good Fortune* in 2006. Then again in *Finding My Elegy*, published by HMH in 2012. Reprinted by permission of Curtis Brown, Ltd.

Aldo Leopold, "April: Sky Dance: Wildlife Conservation on the Farm, an unpaginated collection of reprints from Wisconsin Agriculturist and Farmer, c. September 1941"; *A Sand County Almanac, and Sketches Here and There* (New York: Oxford University Press, 1949); illustrations by Charles W. Schwartz. Reprinted by permission of Informa Business Media, Inc., publisher of Wisconsin Agriculturist.

Meriwether Lewis and William Clark, from *Journals of the Lewis and Clark Expedition*, ed. Gary E. Moulton (Lincoln: University of Nebraska Press, 1983–2004).

Barry Lopez, from *Desert Notes: Reflections in the Eye of a Raven* (Kansas City, MO: Sheed, Andrews & McMeel Publishing, 1976). Copyright © by Barry Lopez. Reprinted by permission of SLL/Sterling Lord Literistic, Inc.

David Tomas Martinez, "Of Mockingbirds," *Hustle* (Louisville: Sarabande Books, 2014). Copyright © 2014 by David Tomas Martinez. Reprinted with the permission of The Permissions Company, Inc., on behalf of Sarabande Books, Inc., www.sarabandebooks.org.

Faith McNulty, from *The Wildlife Stories of Faith McNulty* (New York: Doubleday, 1980). Copyright © by Faith McNulty. Reprinted by permission of Katy Keiffer.

Herman Melville, "The Man-of-War Hawk," *John Marr and Other Sailors* (New York: De Vinne Press, 1888). "The Blue-Bird" (written late 1880s), first published posthumously in *Weeds and Wildings, chiefly: with a Rose or Two,* in the English edition of Melville's work, ed. Raymond Weaver (London: Constable, 1924).

Florence A. Merriam, from *Birds Through an Opera-Glass* (Boston: Houghton Mifflin Company, 1889).

W. S. Merwin, "Unknown Bird," *The Pupil* (New York: Alfred A. Knopf, 2001). Copyright © 2001 by W. S. Merwin. Used by permission of Alfred A. Knopf, an imprint of the Knopf Doubleday Publishing Group, a division of Penguin Random House LLC. All rights reserved.

Marianne Moore, "The Frigate Pelican," *Collected Poems* (New York: Scribner, 1951). Copyright © 1935 by Marianne Moore, renewed 1963 by Marianne Moore and T. S. Eliot. Reprinted with the permission of Scribner, a division of Simon & Schuster, Inc. All rights reserved.

John Muir, from *The Story of My Boyhood and Youth* (Boston: Houghton Mifflin and Company, 1913). From *My First Summer in the Sierra* (Boston: Houghton Mifflin and Company, 1911).

Ogden Nash, "Up from the Egg: The Confessions of a Nuthatch Avoider," *You Can't Get There from Here* (Boston: Little, Brown, 1957). Copyright © 1957 by Ogden Nash, renewed. Reprinted by permission of Curtis Brown, Ltd.

Duane Niatum, "Snowy Owl near Ocean Shores," *Drawings of the Song Animals: New and Selected Poems* (Seattle: Holy Cow! Press, 1991). Copyright © 1991 by Duane Niatum. Reprinted with the permission of The Permissions Company, Inc., on behalf of Holy Cow! Press, www.holycowpress.org.

Theodore Roosevelt, from *An Autobiography* (New York: Macmillan Company, 1913).

Carl Sandburg, "Purple Martins," *Smoke and Steel* (New York: Harcourt, Brace and Howe, 1920).

This material is used by permission of Ohio University Press, www.ohioswallow.com.

Noah Strycker, from *Birding without Borders* (Boston: Houghton Mifflin Harcourt, 2017). Copyright © 2017 by Noah Strycker. Reprinted by permission of Houghton Mifflin Harcourt Publishing Company. All rights reserved.

May Swenson, "Waterbird," *In Other Words* (New York: Alfred A. Knopf, 1987). Copyright © 1987 by May Swenson. Used with permission of The Literary Estate of May Swenson.

Edwin Way Teale, from *Autumn across America* (New York: Dodd, Mead and Company, 1956). Copyright © by the University of Connecticut. Used with permission.

Henry David Thoreau, from *The Journal of Henry David Thoreau*, 14 volumes, ed. Bradford Torrey and Francis H. Allen (Boston: Houghton Mifflin Company, 1906). Used in consultation with *The Writings of Henry D. Thoreau*, 18 volumes (Princeton: Princeton University Press, 1971, 1974, 1976, 1982, 1983, 1985, 1991, 1993, 1997, 2001, 2002, 2004, 2008, 2009, 2013, 2018). Copyright © by Princeton University Press.

Tigua "The Mocking-Bird's Song," from Alice C. Fletcher, *Indian Story and Song from North America* (Boston: Small, Maynard, 1900).

Pamela Uschuk, "Snow Goose Migration at Tule Lake," *Scattered Risks* (San Antonio: Wings Press, 2005). Copyright © by Pamela Uschuk. Also appeared in *Without Birds, Without Flowers, Without Trees* (Chico, CA: Flume Press, 1990). Used by permission of the author.

Sidney Wade, "Indigo Bunting," *Bird Book* (Portland, OR: Atelier26 Books, 2017). Copyright © 2017 by Sidney Wade. Used by permission of the author.

David Wagoner, "Kingfisher," *Traveling Light: Collected and New Poems* (Champaign: University of Illinois Press, 1999). Copyright © 1999 by David Wagoner. Used with permission of the University of Illinois Press.

Robert Penn Warren, "Redwing Blackbirds," *Rumor Verified* (New York: Random House, 1981). Copyright © by Robert Penn Warren. Reprinted by permission of William Morris Endeavor.

John Hall Wheelock, "The Fish-Hawk," *The Black Panther* (New York: Charles Scribner's Sons, 1922).

E. B. White, "A Listener's Guide to the Birds," *Poems and Sketches of E. B. White* (New York: Harper & Row, 1981). Copyright © 1959 by E. B. White. Reprinted by permission of ICM Partners.

Walt Whitman, from *Specimen Days & Collect* (Philadelphia: David McKay, 1882–83).

Richard Wilbur, "A Barred Owl," *Mayflies: New Poems and Translations* (Boston: Houghton Mifflin Harcourt, 2000). Copyright © 2000 by Richard Wilbur. Reprinted by permission of Houghton Mifflin Harcourt Publishing Company. All rights reserved.

C. K. Williams, "Blackbird," *Wait* (New York: Farrar, Straus and Giroux, 2010). Copyright © 2010 by C. K. Williams. Reprinted by permission of Farrar, Straus and Giroux.

Index

This book is set in 10 point ITC New Baskerville Pro,
one of many contemporary type families based on the work of
English printer John Baskerville (1706–1775), whose projects included
books for the University of Cambridge, most famously a folio Bible
in 1763. ITC New Baskerville is a modern interpretation of
Baskerville's style, designed by John Quaranda in the late
twentieth century for International Typeface Corporation.

The chapter titles and section heads are set in boldface variations
of Baskerville Original, designed by the Storm Type Foundry in Prague
to "preserve the spirit" of John Baskerville's original typeface while
creating a simpler, more elegant font than other available
Baskerville bold complements. Subheads and running heads
are in Trade Gothic LT, a sans serif type designed by
Jackson Burke during the 1950s for Linotype.

The paper is an acid-free Forest Stewardship Council–certified stock
that exceeds the requirements for permanence of the American
National Standards Institute. The binding material is Arrestox,
a cotton-based cloth with an aqueous acrylic coating
manufactured by Holliston, Church Hill, Tennessee.
Text design and composition, as well as the jacket design,
are by Gopa & Ted2, Inc., Albuquerque, New Mexico.
Printing and binding by McNaughton & Gunn,
Saline, Michigan.